THE FRANK P. PISKOR COLLECTION OF ROBERT FROST

Special Collections
Owen D. Young Library
St. Lawrence University
Canton, New York 13617

1993

ISBN 0-09634028-1-1

TABLE OF CONTENTS

THE FRANK P. PISKOR COLLECTION OF ROBERT FROST

Description of the Collection

DR. FRANK P. PISKOR enjoyed a long relationship with Robert Frost, stretching back to Dr. Piskor's student days at Middlebury. Over the years his admiration for Frost's work led him to collect not only editions of Frost's own books, but also an extensive library of secondary sources, both books and periodical articles. The result of this passion for Frostiana is the Frank P. Piskor Collection of Robert Frost, formally presented to St. Lawrence University in October 1993.

The collection contains first editions of all Frost's books, as well as those of his friends, Edward Thomas and Philip Booth. In addition to the periodical articles about Frost and his work, the non-book section of the collection contains materials which illuminate Frost's connections with a number of educational institutions. In the correspondence section are previously unpublished reminiscences by those who had contact with Frost and his wife, Elinor, and the section on works about Frost contains holograph poems honoring Frost, written by well-known contemporaries. The Frost family photo album provides a visual record to supplement the written materials, and the tapes enable the user to hear Frost's poems read by himself and others.

With very little Frost manuscript material, the collection is of minimal use to scholars wishing to sift through Frost's own papers. However, for those interested in public reaction to Frost, or seeking ephemeral Frost items with limited printings, or wishing to see how an aficionado goes about building a collection on a living author, this collection is a rich resource.

Use of the Collection

The Frank Piskor Collection of Robert Frost is the exclusive property of St. Lawrence University. It is available for use by any researcher, without special permission, from 8:30 a.m. to 5:00 p.m. on weekdays.

Plans for publication of any material from the collection should be discussed with the curator of special collections, and credit should be given St. Lawrence University in any written materials making use of information from this collection.

The user should be aware that literary property rights to this collection are not held by St. Lawrence. According to law, the writer of a letter or unpublished manuscript has the sole right to publish the contents thereof, unless he or she specifically gives up that right. Regardless of the physical ownership of the manuscript itself, that right remains with the writer and his or her legal heirs. Therefore, it is the responsibility of an author to secure the permission of the owner of the literary property rights when quoting any unpublished material from the collection.

Lynn Ekfelt
Curator of Special Collections

ACKNOWLEDGEMENTS AND APPRECIATIONS

THIS IS A STATEMENT of appreciation as well as acknowledgement. The exercise of helping organize the materials for this bibliography has taught me how critical the devotion of friends and colleagues has been to the development of this collection and the great number who became involved over many years.

Chancellor Emeritus of Syracuse University William Pearson Tolley's special contributions to the building of the collection are mentioned in my introduction. Equally important has been the unflagging support and patience of my wife, Anne, and my daughters Joanne and Nancy. I am pleased to have Anne's college, Mount Holyoke, and Joanne's professional home, Phillips Exeter Academy, represented. The inspiring leadership, superb organizing ability and creative energy of Richard J. Kuhta, director of the Owen D. Young Library, has been indispensable. My debt to Lesley Frost Ballantine is very great and my association with her deeply treasured — a family association which I am now enjoying with her daughter, Lesley Lee Francis. To all these special people a special thank you.

This publication itself would never have seen the light of day if it were not for my library colleagues and the team that produced this bibliography. Special thanks are in order to the two individuals responsible for compiling the entries for this publication: Henry Emmans, former ODYer and now cataloger at SUNY Oswego, who has worked on other library publications but exceeded all expectations on this one, despite the drawbacks of a three-hour commute to the collection and a broken ankle around deadline time; and to Lynn Ekfelt, curator of special collections, who somehow managed to create bibliographic order out of the mountain of non-book material which enriches this collection, working nights and weekends to do so. With their teammates in the cataloging department of the library, everything was prepared for press in a timely manner.

My thanks to Jim Benvenuto, designer, for his eye and expertise in making this bibliography the physical object it is — a thing of beauty to my eye. Theresa Stark was my secretary in the office of the president at the time of my retirement and it was my good fortune to work closely with her again on this project. I thank her for finding titles and getting printouts when we needed them, keeping me supplied with coffee, making corrections to the text, and generally keeping me on track as she always has for many years.

The richness and variety of the collection is the result in large measure of the interest of friends and colleagues at Syracuse University, Dartmouth, Middlebury and St. Lawrence, as well as Robert Frost associates, friends and admirers in the United States and Great Britain. At Syracuse, David Tatham's contributions particularly to the New Hampshire years and the English years of the Frost family stand out as one of a kind. Donald Ely's avid development of the audio portion of the collection was accomplished single-handedly, and the results of the scouting of Howard Applegate and Martin Bush are clearly evident throughout the materials. The then poet-in-residence at Syracuse, Philip Booth, who is represented in the collection; professors Walter Sutton and Antje Lemke (friend of the Frost photographer Clara Sipprell); and the late Lester G. Wells, first director of special collections at Syracuse, provided invaluable advice and resources. My secretary in Syracuse, the late Marion Borst, developed the only organized card file on the materials in existence, truly a labor of love, done outside of office hours on her own time. Her work was carried on by Isabel Pearce Shake.

Herbert F. West, professor of English at Dartmouth, and Edward Connery Latham, Dartmouth librarian, were both major builders and boosters of my effort. Mr. Latham was responsible for the inclusion of my English edition of "Masque of Reason" in "The Robert Frost 100" traveling exhibition.

My Middlebury College friends were a small but choice and influential group. Harry Goddard Owen's contribution early on is recognized in the introduction. The inspiration of Professor Reginald L. Cook, my professor of American literature, is evident throughout. Storrs Lee and George Huban, leaders in Middlebury's communications and media relations in different periods of the college, stayed close to this effort as did my chef boss, Edward J. "Eddie" Doucette. Middlebury alumna Corrine Davids, who established their fine Hawkins-Frost collection, was a good friend.

Kathleen Morrison, Mr. Frost's longtime personal secretary and confidante; the late Lawrence Thompson, his biographer; and Cynthia S. Walsh of the Hampshire Bookshop and Bacon Collamore, whose collection now resides at Trinity (Connecticut) College, contributed special items and advice at the asking. I have previously acknowledged my debt to Betram Ruta and Marguerite Colfin, unique booksellers both, and I do now to Herman Cohen of the Chiswick Bookshop (New York) and James F. Carr of Carr Books and Antiques. My wife's aunt Helen B. Calder is responsible for much judicious newspaper clipping, especially from *The Christian Science Monitor*, which has enriched our resources.

When I arrived at St. Lawrence the heart of the collection was established. I was fortunate for the interest early on of Ann Kray Kirkpatrick, who took over the pioneering work of Marion Borst at Syracuse. My executive assistant at that time,

David Powers, used his photographic talents to broaden the collection's coverage in photography. Thurlow Cannon did much to publicize the collection and the Frost connection with St. Lawrence. Francis Murphy applied his audio talents and extended the Syracuse work of Donald Ely. Lastly, Allen P. Splete literally packed up the collection for transfer from Syracuse to St. Lawrence, and helped unpack it when he joined the administration at St. Lawrence!

One final note. St. Lawrence alumni have not only expressed interest but served as scouts with enthusiasm. They are too numerous to mention but I would be remiss if I did not acknowledge Mary Martin '43, Robert A. Cushman '32, Emerson Laughland '36, the late Marion Van Dyke Stone '25, Professor Rutherford E. Delmage '32 and the late Florence "Billie" Martin Johnson '19 for their interest, suggestions and gifts.

Frank P. Piskor

Frank P. Piskor

INTRODUCTION

PRIVATE BOOK COLLECTIONS are unique creations and the Robert Frost Collection at St. Lawrence is no exception. As I have tried to indicate in my appreciations and acknowledgements, it was assembled by many hands and supportive friends, and with the invaluable professional help of the late Bertram Rota of Bertram Rota Ltd. of London and the late Marguerite Cohn of House of Books Ltd. of New York City. It is a comprehensive collection accumulated over a lifetime between 1935 and 1993, and contains all of Mr. Frost's first editions, first printings of many poems including all of his Christmas poems, his lectures, introductions to the books of others, and books about him and his work, as well as articles and reviews (many of them now out of print) of interest to students and scholars. The first editions include English and American firsts, as well as variants. Many contain inscriptions, notations and poems written out by the poet. Translations into other languages have been deliberately sought out, as have photographs, recordings and tapes of Frost readings and commentaries. The collection has a fine core of rarities, some as a result of gifts received from the poet. Hopefully, undergraduate and faculty scholarship will be stimulated and the reading of Mr. Frost's poetry enhanced.

I purchased Frost books as I could afford them as early as 1935 (the end of my sophomore year at Middlebury) not as a collector but because I enjoyed the poetry. It was Chancellor William Pearson Tolley of Syracuse University, a longtime book collector, who convinced me to conceive of my Frost library as a collection and work on extending and refining it. He advanced the effort with several impressive gifts of first editions from his personal library.

When the collection became a reality, I had no idea, of course, that St. Lawrence might be in my future or for that matter that Elinor Miriam White, one of its distinguished 1895 graduates and a contemporary of Owen D. Young was Mrs. Robert Frost. Once St. Lawrence became part of my life, I harbored dreams of establishing a Frost Family Collection in honor of Elinor White Frost and shared this dream with the Frosts' oldest daughter, Lesley. We agreed to join in such a project in principle, Lesley's enthusiasm heightened by her visit to a Frost Family Exhibition at St. Lawrence in May of 1971. Unfortunately, her untimely death precluded bringing our plans to fruition.

I refer above to 1935. That summer I was hired as a kitchen assistant by the Director of the Bread Loaf School of English, Harry Goddard Owen, who had also been my professor of English at Middlebury during my freshman year. Everyone in the kitchen worked hard (cooking was done on wood-burning stoves!) but those interested were encouraged to take advantage of lectures and readings at the Bread Loaf School. I attended my first Frost reading that summer and can still hear it and see it as if had occurred yesterday. It was my kind of poetry. I asked Dean Owen if he would introduce me to Mr. Frost so that he could sign a book of his for me. I was introduced, "West-running Brook" was signed, and an invitation to call on Mr. Frost at his cabin issued. I visited him there that summer and, thanks to Kathleen Morrison, his faithful secretary, for the next three summers. The visits remain a vivid memory. We enjoyed great talk. (Unfortunately, I was not astute enough to take pictures or make notes.)

"West-running Brook" is a special treasure in this collection [see photo, p. 35], because it was signed in 1935 at Bread Loaf and again on April 21, 1959, on the poet's visit to Syracuse University and to our home after the academic convocation. That visit rekindled a friendship which kept on growing until his death.

Robert Frost loved all kinds of people and especially students, college students in particular. He relished his role as teacher in a classroom or on the podium. On a visit to Amherst, when the topic turned to education he said to me, "Education is hanging around in the right places and the right people until you get an idea! Students are good people to hang around." That the poet had a weakness for student audiences is amply demonstrated by his itineraries. This collection reflects that. Recall his advice in his political pastoral "Build Soil": "Join the United States, and join the family, but not much in between, unless a college."

Although basically sympathetic to the college communities, he held reservations about their ability to accommodate a budding poet's needs. He once wrote, "School and college have been conducted with the almost express purpose of keeping him busy with something else till the danger of his ever creating anything is past. Their motto has been, the muses find some mischief still for idle hands to do. No one is asking to see poetry regularized in courses and directed by coaches like sociology and football. It must remain a theft to retain its savor. But it does seem as if it could be a little more connived at than it is. I for one should be in favor of the colleges setting the expectation of poetry forward a few years (the way the clocks are set forward in May), so as to get the young poets started earlier in the morning before the freshness dries off. Just setting the expectation of poetry forward might be all that was needed to give us our proportional number of poets to Congressmen." (Introduction to *Dartmouth Verse*, June 1925.) In this collection, the works of two young poets, Edward Thomas and Philip Booth, each a friend in a different period of Frost's life, are both represented in some depth. Others could be.

“West-running Brook” has another distinction — a book jacket with some definitions of poetry by Robert Frost appearing for the first time. It is a succinct summing up worthy of periodic review, reflection and study. In these pages I shall quote only the last paragraph of the flyleaf:

> A poem begins with a lump in the throat;
> a home-sickness or a love-sickness. It is
> reaching-out toward expression; an effort
> to find fulfillment. A complete poem is one
> where an emotion has found its thought and
> the thought has found the words.

Simplicity capable of capturing and retaining every relevant subtlety in a situation is a hallmark in all Frost poetry. Magically, it helps us see what has always been there but what more often than not we have consistently missed. One learns to come to Frost’s poems because there is always something new to discover in them. As my one-time professor of American literature, Reginald L. Cook, has written, “Like the best of poetry, they are rich in multiple choices...there is no expectation of apocalyptic vision...only cautious, teasing, penetrating insights.” (*Massachusetts Review*, Winter 1963, p. 245.) The overwhelming stream of critical writing about Frost in this collection confirms Professor Cook’s insights.

Eventually the time arrives for a private collection to be sold or placed in a new home. My family and I are pleased that our affection for St. Lawrence made that decision an easy one.

Frank P. Piskor

A FROST CHRONOLOGY

1874 Born March 26 to William Prescott and Isabelle Moodie Frost in San Francisco.

1885 William Prescott Frost dies of tuberculosis. Isabelle moves with her children to New Hampshire, where she becomes a school teacher.

1892 Frost and Elinor Miriam White are co-valedictorians of their high-school class in Lawrence, Massachusetts.
Frost begins college classes at Dartmouth and Elinor at St. Lawrence.
Frost drops out of Dartmouth before the semester ends.

1894 Sells his first professional poem, "My Butterfly," to the *New York Independent* for its November 8 issue.

1895 Marries Elinor White December 19.

1896 Elliott Frost born September 25.

1897 Frost enters Harvard as a special student, then withdraws after eighteen months, without taking a degree.

1899 Lesley Frost born April 28.

1900 Elliott dies July 8.
The family moves to Derry, NH, to live on a farm owned by Frost's grandfather.

1902 Carol Frost born May 27.

1903 Irma Frost born June 27.

1905 Marjorie Frost born March 29.

1906 Frost accepts a part-time teaching job at Pinkerton Academy.

1907 Elinor Bettina Frost born June 18; dies June 21.

1911 The family moves to Plymouth, NH, where Frost teaches at the Plymouth Normal School.

1912 The family moves to England.

1913 *A Boy's Will* published in England in April.
Ezra Pound publishes the first important American review of a Frost book in the May issue of *Poetry* magazine.

1914 *North of Boston*.

1915 The family returns to the United States.
Phi Beta Kappa Poet at Tufts.

1916 Phi Beta Kappa Poet at Harvard.
Elected to National Institute of Arts and Letters.

1922 Levinson prize (*Poetry* magazine).

1923 *New Hampshire*.

1924 Pulitzer Prize for *New Hampshire*.

1928 *West-running Brook*.

1930 *Collected Poems of Robert Frost*.
Elected to American Academy of Arts and Letters.

1931 Pulitzer Prize for *Collected Poems of Robert Frost*.
Russell Loines Poetry Prize (National Institute of Arts and Letters).

1932 Phi Beta Kappa Poet at Columbia.

1934 Marjorie dies of puerperal fever.

1936 *A Further Range.*

1937 Pulitzer Prize for *A Further Range.*

1938 Elinor dies of a heart attack and cancer.

1939 Gold Medal for Poetry (National Institute of Arts and Letters).

1940 Carol commits suicide.
Phi Beta Kappa Poet at Tufts.

1941 Phi Beta Kappa Poet at William and Mary.
Phi Beta Kappa Poet at Harvard.
Gold Medal (Poetry Society of America).

1942 *A Witness Tree.*

1943 *Come In and Other Poems.*
Pulitzer Prize for *A Witness Tree.*

1945 *A Masque of Reason.*

1947 *A Masque of Mercy.*
Steeple Bush.

1949 Gold Medal (Limited Editions Club).

1951 *The Road Not Taken.*

1953 American Academy of Poets Award.

1954 Sent to Brazil by the State Department as a delegate to the World Congress of Writers.

1956 Medal of Honor (New York University).

1958 Appointed Consultant in Poetry to the Library of Congress.
Huntington Hartford Foundation award.
Emerson-Thoreau Medal (American Academy of Arts & Sciences).
Medal for Achievement in the Arts (Harvard).
Gold Medal (Poetry Society of America).

1959 *You Come Too.*

1961 Participates in the inaugural ceremony for John F. Kennedy.

1962 Congressional Gold Medal.
Edward MacDowell Medal.
Sent on an official mission to the Soviet Union.
In the Clearing.

1963 Bollingen Prize for Poetry.
Dies January 29.

WORKS BY ROBERT FROST

All items are located in the
Frank and Anne Piskor Special Collections Area.

Note: Numbers at the upper right corner of the entry refer to page numbers in the following four standard bibliographies of Frost, one for Thomas, and one for Robinson from which the edition information was taken.

C = *Robert Frost: A Bibliography* by William Branford Shubrick Clymer and Charles R. Green. Amherst, MA: Jones Library, Inc., 1937.

Crane = *Robert Frost: A Descriptive Catalogue of Books and Manuscripts in the Clifton Waller Barrett Library, University of Virginia* compiled by Joan St. C. Crane. Charlottesville, VA: Published for the Associates of the University of Virginia Library by the University Press of Virginia, c1974.

Eckert = *Edward Thomas: A Biography and a Bibliography* by Robert P. Eckert. London: J. M. Dent & Sons Ltd., 1937.

Ewert = *Robert Frost New Hampshire* by William B. Ewert. Durham: Friends of the Library, Univ. of New Hampshire, c1976.

Hogan = *A Bibliography of Edwin Arlington Robinson* by Charles Beecher Hogan. New Haven: Yale University Press, 1936.

Mertins = *The Intervals of Robert Frost: A Critical Bibliography* by Louis and Esther Mertins. Berkeley: University of California Press, 1947.

[2] *Aforesaid.* Crane A37

New York: Henry Holt and Company, 1954.

First edition. Limited to 650 numbered copies signed by Robert Frost. Library's copy is number 558. Binding: gray-green linen cloth. A dark green panel stamped on the front cover, lettering gilt-stamped within a single gilt rule frame. Spine with gilt-stamped lettering reading from top to bottom within a dark green panel with a single gilt rule. Back cover blank. In a board slipcase covered with blue-green paper, white paper label on spine lettered in blue-green within a blue-green rule frame, reading from top to bottom. Cream wove paper, all edges trimmed. Endpapers of blue-green laid paper. Publication coincided with the celebration of the author's eightieth birthday.

Rare Book Room PS3511.R94 A8 1954

The Augustan Books of Poetry. C:58-59

London: Ernest Benn, Ltd., [1932]

First edition. No binding, red linen covers pasted over original cover sheets with cut out panel in the front cover to allow "Robert Frost" to show through. All edges trimmed. Copy 1 is signed by Frost on the front cover. Copy 2 is signed by Frost on p. 5.

Rare Book Room PS3511.R94 A6 1932 (2 copies)

A Boy's Will. C:20-21

London: David Nutt, 1913.

First edition. Binding: brown pebbled cloth; front cover bordered with a blind rule and lettered in gilt. Spine and back cover blank. All edges untrimmed. Copy 1 is first issue in brown leather backed slipcase. Publishers complementary stamp on title page and original page and original price stamp. Copy selected as an alternate for *Frost 100*. Copy 2 is Binding D in a green cloth slipcase. Heavy cream-colored paper wrappers; front cover printed like first issue but in black and without border. All edges trimmed. No endpapers, wrappers glued to sheets at spine. Lettering is quite different from that on first issue, as are the ornaments. Signed by Frost.

Rare Book Room PS3511.R94 B6 1913 (2 copies)

A Boy's Will. C:27-28

New York: Henry Holt and Company, 1915.

First American edition. Binding: blue cloth; front cover stamped in gilt with double-line rectangle, lettered within. Spine stamped in gilt. Back cover blank. Top edges trimmed, fore and bottom edges untrimmed. Endpapers cream. Copy 2 is first edition, first issue. 750 copies. Gift of Wm. P. Tolley. Inscribed by Frost on front flyleaf "This very early. On page VII it reads, 'he is resolved to become inteligable [sic] at least to himself,' on the very next page, 'and to know definitely what he thinks about the soul.' Robert Frost. Attention of Frank Piskor." In publisher's box. Copy 3 is First American edition, first issue. Copy 4 is First American edition, second issue. Inscribed by Frost: "Wilmington, 1931". Misprint corrected on page 14.

Rare Book Room PS3511.R94 B6 1915 (3 copies, numbered 2-4)

A Boy's Will. C:62-63

New York: Henry Holt, 1934.

Second American Edition. Binding: tan cloth with printed brown panel on front cover on which are stamped in gilt three scythes crossed. Spine has printed brown label lettered in gilt from bottom to top. Back cover blank. All edges trimmed. Endpapers white. Dust jacket. Inscribed by Frost: "For the Piskor's [sic] to keep on keeping on my authority, Syracuse April 21, 1959."

Rare Book Room PS3511.R94 B6 1934

A BOY'S WILL

BY

ROBERT FROST

LONDON
DAVID NUTT
17 GRAPE STREET, NEW OXFORD STREET, W.C.
1913

A Boy's Will. London: David Nutt, 1913. First edition, first issue. Frost's first book.

Collected Poems. C:52

New York: Random House, 1930.

First edition. Limited to 1,000 copies signed by Frost. This copy is one of an unnumbered set of overruns in a special binding. Binding: light tan buckram. Front and back covers blank. Brown label bordered with a single gilt line sunk in panel on spine, lettered in gilt. Top edges trimmed and gilded, fore and bottom edges untrimmed. Mould-made paper. Endpapers white. Included in AIGA 50 Best Books of the Year.

Rare Book Room PS3511 .R94 1930

[4] *Collected Poems of Robert Frost.* Mertins 73-74

New York: Halcyon House, [1939]

First Halcyon House edition, third printing. Binding: green cloth with gold lettering on black panel on spine. Front cover with indented facsimile of Frost's signature. Top edge trimmed and stained dark green, fore and bottom edges untrimmed.

Rare Book Room PS3511 .R94 1939a c.2

Collected Poems of Robert Frost.

Garden City, N.Y.: Garden City Publishing Company, [c1942]

Dust jacket.

Rare Book Room PS3511 .R94 1942

Collected Poems of Robert Frost, 1939. Crane A23

New York: Henry Holt and Company, 1939.

First edition. Binding: beige medium linen cloth. Within a red-brown panel on the front cover, a gilt stamped version of J. J. Lankes' title-page vignette of a house. Spine lettered in gilt within a red-brown panel. Back cover blank. White wove paper. Top edge trimmed and stained red-brown, fore-edge uncut, bottom edge rough cut. Endpapers of heavier smooth white wove paper. Copy 2 is signed by Robert Frost.

Rare Book Room PS3511 .R94 1939 c.2

Come In and Other Poems. Crane A26

[New York]: Henry Holt and Company, 1943.

First edition. Binding: cream glazed linen cloth. On front cover is a vignette of a farmhouse stamped in red-brown. Spine stamped in red-brown. Back cover blank. Cream wove paper. All edges trimmed, top edge stained red-brown. Pictorial endpapers printed in colors; a watercolor, signed "J. O'H. Cosgrave II." Copy 1 inscribed "For Joanne & Nancy - from Robert Frost - your friend forever - 1959" [Joanne and Nancy are the daughters of Frank and Ann Piskor]. Dust jacket.

Rare Book Room PS3511.R94 A6 1943 (2 copies)

Come In and Other Poems Crane A26.1

London: Jonathan Cape, 1944.

First English edition. Binding: blue fine linen cloth, covers blank. Spine stamped in gilt and lettered from bottom to top. Cheap white wove paper.

COMPLETE
POEMS
OF
ROBERT
FROST
1949

HENRY HOLT AND COMPANY
NEW YORK

Complete Poems of Robert Frost. New York: Henry Holt, 1949. First trade edition. Inscribed "Robert Frost / to / Frank Piskor / in friendship / April 21, 1959."

Top and fore-edge trimmed, bottom rough-cut. Top edge stained dark blue. Dust jacket.

Rare Book Room PS3511.R94 A6 1944

The Complete Poems of Robert Frost.
Preface by the author; an appreciation by Louis Untermeyer; wood-engravings by Thomas W. Nason; designed by Bruce Rogers.
New York: The Limited Editions Club, 1950.

2 volume edition limited to 1500 copies. Library's copy is number 1339. In original glassine jackets. Signed by Robert Frost, Thomas W. Nason and Bruce Rogers.

Rare Book Room PS3511 .R94 1950 v.1 and 2

 Complete Poems of Robert Frost. Crane A35.2
London: Jonathan Cape, 1951.

First English edition. Binding: blue-green fine linen cloth. Covers blank. Spine stamped in gilt. Dust jacket. White wove paper, all edges trimmed, top edge stained green. Endpapers of heavier white wove paper.

Rare Book Room PS3511 .R94 1951

Complete Poems of Robert Frost, 1949. Crane A35.1
New York: Henry Holt and Company, 1949.

First trade edition. Binding: blue-green linen cloth. Facsimile gilt-stamped signature, 'Robert Frost', on front cover. Spine gilt-stamped. Back cover blank. White wove paper, all edges trimmed. Top edge stained dark green. Endpapers of heavier white wove paper. Dust jacket. Frontispiece inscribed "Robert Frost to Frank Piskor in friendship, April 21, 1959."

Rare Book Room PS3511 .R94 1949a

Conoscenza della Notte e Altre Poesie.
Translated by Giovanni Giudici.
[Torino]: Einaudi, c1965.

Italian and English on alternate pages. Dust jacket.

Rare Book Room PS3511.R94 A55 1965

A Considerable Speck. Crane A24
[S.l.: s.n.], 1939.

First separate edition. Library's copy is one of less than 100 copies printed. Binding: a single folio gathering, 38.7 X 29.5 cm., uncut, on cream wove paper. In slipcase.

Rare Book Room PS3511.R94 C66 1939

The Cow's in the Corn: A One-Act Irish Play in Rhyme. C:49
Gaylordsville, [Conn.]: Slide Mountain Press, 1929.

Edition limited to 91 signed copies. Library's copy is "out of series." Decorated paper-covered boards. Front and back covers blank. White paper label on spine lettered in black italics from bottom to top. All edges untrimmed. No endpapers. Custom made slipcase. The second book published by the Slide Mountain Press. Library's copy is signed by Frost.

Rare Book Room PS3511.R94 C68 1929

A CONSIDERABLE SPECK
ROBERT FROST

A SPECK that would have been beneath my sight
On any but a paper sheet so white
Set off across what I had written there,
And I had idly poised my pen in air
To stop it with a period of ink,
When something strange about it made me think
This was no dust speck by my breathing blown
But unmistakably a living mite
With inclinations it could call its own.
It paused as with suspicion of my pen
And then came racing wildly on again
To where my manuscript was not yet dry,
Then paused again and either drank or smelt–
With horror, for again it turned to fly.
Plainly with an intelligence I dealt.
It seemed too tiny to have room for feet
Yet must have had a set of them complete
To express how much it didn't want to die.
It ran with terror and with cunning crept.
It faltered! I could see it hesitate–
Then in the middle of the open sheet
Cower down in desperation to accept
Whatever I accorded it of fate.
I have none of the tenderer-than-thou
Political collectivistic love
With which the modern world is being swept–
But this poor microscopic item now!
Since it was nothing I knew evil of
I let it lie there till I hope it slept.
I have a mind myself and recognize
Mind where I meet with it in any guise.
No one can know how glad I am to find
On any sheet the least display of mind.

A Considerable Speck. Boston: Dard Hunter Jr., 1939. First edition. Four-page leaflet printed on paper hand made by Hunter and his father.

THE COW'S IN THE CORN

A ONE-ACT IRISH PLAY

IN RHYME

BY

ROBERT FROST

THE SLIDE MOUNTAIN PRESS

GAYLORDSVILLE

MCMXXIX

The Cow's in the Corn. Gaylordsville: Slide Mountain Press, 1929. First separate edition. One of 91 signed by Frost.

[8]

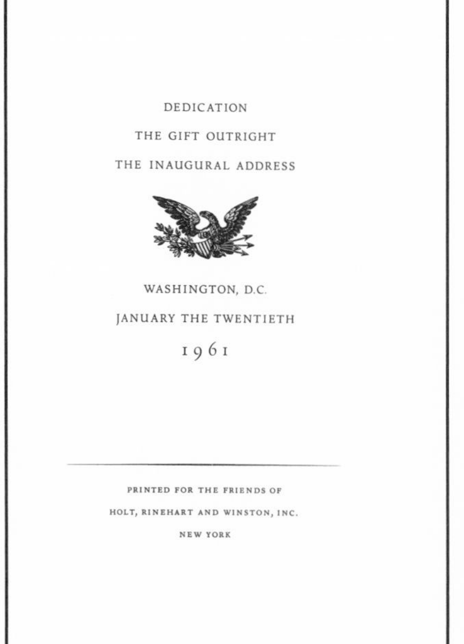

DEDICATION

THE GIFT OUTRIGHT

THE INAUGURAL ADDRESS

WASHINGTON, D.C.

JANUARY THE TWENTIETH

1961

PRINTED FOR THE FRIENDS OF

HOLT, RINEHART AND WINSTON, INC.

NEW YORK

Dedication: The Gift Outright. New York: Spiral Press, 1961. 227/500. Prepared for the inauguration of John F. Kennedy, 35th President of the United States. Kennedy's inaugural address included.

Dedication: The Gift Outright, the Inaugural Address. Crane A40
Typography by Joseph Blumenthal.
Washington, D.C., New York: Printed at the Spiral Press, 1961.

First separate edition. Limited to 500 numbered copies. Library's copy is number 227. Binding: very light brown-gray paper over boards. On the front cover, printed in brown-gray, is the seal of the President of the United States, engraved in wood by Fritz Kredel and printed from the block. Spine lettered from top to bottom. Back cover blank. "Printed for the Friends of Holt, Rinehart and Winston, Inc." Contains President Kennedy's inaugural address.

Rare Book Room PS3511.R94 D42 1961

Family Letters of Robert and Elinor Frost.
Edited by Arnold Grade. Foreword by Lesley Frost.
Albany, N.Y.: State University of New York Press, 1972.

First edition. Copy 3 has inscription to Frank Piskor by Lesley Frost Ballantine. Dust jacket.

Rare Book Room PS3511.R94 Z52 1972 c.3

THE FOUR BELIEFS
BY ROBERT FROST

The Four Beliefs

One is the self-belief, which is a knowledge that you don't want to tell other people about because you cannot prove that you know. You are saying nothing about it till you see.

The love belief has that same shyness. It knows it cannot tell; only the outcome will tell.

And the national belief we enter into socially with each other to bring on the future of the country. We cannot tell some people what it is we believe, partly because they are too stupid to understand, partly because we are too proudly vague to explain. And anyway we are not talking until we know more, until we have something to show.

And then the one in every work of art. This is not of cunning and craft, mind you, but of art. You say as you go more than you even hoped you were going to be able to say, and come with surprise to an end that you foreknew only with some sort of emotion. You have believed the thing into existence.

And then finally there is the relation we enter into with God to believe the future in. That by which we believe the future in is our belief in God.

ROBERT FROST

Four Beliefs. Hanover, NH: n.d. (1943). 4 pp. First separate appearance of this prose article. Annotated by Frost in October 1962. This may be one of the last items Frost inscribed; it was signed while he was in the hospital and he died within 60 days. "To Frank Piskor / There Seem to be Five. Maybe it should be / added that we may be blocked in any or all of the first / four and still come through to the last. The force that believes / the future in and even the hereafter in." Gift of Anne C. Piskor.

The Four Beliefs. Crane D6

Typography by Ray Nash; wood engravings by J. J. Lankes.

Hanover, N.H.: R. Nash, Graphic Arts Workshop, Dartmouth College, [194-]

An edition of 250 copies of which 200 were destined for use in "A Miscellany Of The Society of Printers (not issued). Excerpt from *Education by poetry - a meditative monologue*, an address given to the Amherst Alumni Council, November 15, 1930. Copy 1 inscribed by the author with special annotations added on Oct. 1962. This may be one of the last items Frost inscribed. This copy is the gift of Anne C. Piskor.

Rare Book Room PS3511.R94 F6 (2 copies)

[10] *From Snow to Snow.* C:70-71

New York: Henry Holt and Company, [1936]

First edition. One of 300 copies issued as a special issue of the Hampshire Bookshop with the title page "The Hampshire Bookshop 1916-1936, Twentieth Anniversary." Binding: mottled light tan folded paper covers. Front cover bordered with gray blue triple rule and lettered in blue. White antique laid paper, wire stitched and trimmed. Signed by Frost.

Rare Book Room PS3511.R94 F7 1936b

The Hampshire Bookshop

1916 - 1936

TWENTIETH ANNIVERSARY WEEK

Robert Frost

Guest of Honor

on the evening of

April 16, 1936

From Snow to Snow. New York: Henry Holt, 1936. First edition, first issue. Signed. One of 300 copies issued as a special issue of the Hampshire Bookshop.

From Snow to Snow. C:70-71

New York: Henry Holt, [c1936]

First edition. Without the tipped in Hampshire Bookshop sheet. Copy 3 binding: mottled light tan folded paper covers. Front cover bordered with gray blue triple rule and lettered in blue. White antique laid paper, wire stitched and trimmed. Copies 4 & 5 binding: rough tan linen cloth. Lettered in dark brown on the front cover, spine blank. Stitched at center fold. Mottled light tan endpapers. All edges trimmed. Copies 3 and 5 are signed by author.

Rare Book Room PS3511.R94 F7 1936 (3 copies, numbered 3-5)

A Further Range: Book Six. C:75-76

New York: Henry Holt and Company, [c1936]

Edition limited to 803 numbered copies signed by Robert Frost. Copy 1 is number 130 and copy 2 is number 65. Binding: light tan coarse linen speckled with brown. Front and back covers blank. Brown leather label on spine lettered in gold from bottom to top, bordered with single gold rule. Slip case: brown paper covered cardboard, no printing or lettering. Top edges trimmed and stained brown. Fore and bottom edges untrimmed. Copy 1 includes Earl J. Bernheimer's traditional 3 cent stamp and an order slip advertising leaflet from the dedication page initialed "R.F." Signed by Frost for Bernheimer.

Rare Book Room PS3511.R94 F8 1936c (2 copies)

A Further Range: Book Six. C:72-73

New York: Henry Holt and Company, [c1936]

First trade edition. Binding: red buckram; front cover stamped in gilt within a triple-rule gilt panel. Spine lettered in gilt from bottom to top. Back cover blank. At head of title: Book six. Top edges trimmed and stained red, fore and bottom edges untrimmed. Endpapers white. Copies 2 and 4 have dust jackets. Copy 6 has been rebound in blue half-leather with title stamped in gilt on spine.

Rare Book Room PS3511 .R94 F8 1936 (5 copies, numbered 2-6)

A Further Range: Book Six. Crane A21.2

London: Jonathan Cape, [1937]

First English edition. Binding: fine blue linen cloth. Covers plain, spine stamped in gilt. Top edge trimmed, fore-edge uncut, bottom edge rough-cut. Endpapers of rougher cream wove paper. At head of title: Book six. Both copies have dust jackets.

Rare Book Room PS3511.R94 F8 1937 (2 copies)

Gedichte.

Edited by Eva Hesse with translations by Paul Celan and others.

Ebenhausen bei München: Langewiesche-Brandt, c1963.

German and English. Includes biographical sketch (p. 96-97). Dust jacket.

Rare Book Room PS3511.R94 A17 1963

Gesammelte Gedichte.

Translated by Alexander von Bernus and others.

Mannheim: Kessler Verlag, [1952]

German translation of *The Collected Poems of Robert Frost.* First time Frost was translated into a foreign language.

Rare Book Room PS3511.R94 A4215 1952

[12] *The Gold Hesperidee.* C:67-68

Cortland, N. Y.: The Bibliophile Press, 1935.

First edition. Binding: tan paper wrappers, sewn with heavy brown cotton thread, front cover bordered with black rule and lettered in black. Back cover blank. All edges trimmed. Five hundred copies of the first state were printed; all but 37 (unnumbered) were withdrawn due to error on p. 7. After the second issue sold out, 67 copies of the withdrawn first issue were released and stamped "English" under "Copy Number." Copy 1 is first state with "A" on the copyright page and with the second line from the bottom on p. 7 consisting of 9 words. Copy 2 is stamped "English" under copy number. Frost has crossed out in the foreword "one of his favorites" and initialed it at the top. Mint in tan clamshell slipcase.

The Gold Hesperidee. Cortland, NY: The Bibliophile Press, 1935. First state. In the foreword Frost has crossed out "one of his favorites" and initialed the deletion.

Rare Book Room PS3511.R94 G6 1935 (2 copies)

Hard Not to Be King. Crane A36

New York: House of Books, Ltd., 1951.

First separate edition. Limited to 300 numbered copies signed by Robert Frost. Copy is number 196. Binding: deep blue fine linen cloth. Front cover stamped in gilt. Spine stamped in gilt reading from bottom to top. Back cover blank. Cream laid paper, all edges trimmed. Endpapers cream laid paper.

Rare Book Room PS3511.R94 H3 1951

How to Read a Poem.
[Lancaster, N.H.]: New England Books, [1975]

Small-Tall Editions. Limited to 1000 copies. From an interview by Myron Magnet and George Trow originally published in *The Pendulum* for October-November 1960 at The Phillips Exeter Academy.

Rare Book Room PS3511.R94 H68

How to Read a Poem. Lancaster, NH: Stinehour Press, 1975. Limited to 1,000 copies. [Shown actual size.]

In the Clearing. Crane A41
New York: Holt, Rinehart and Winston, 1962.

Edition limited to 1500 numbered copies signed by Robert Frost. Copy 1 is number 1143 and library's copy 2 is number 869. Binding: light brown linen cloth. Covers blank. Spine with lettering stamped in gilt, reading from top to bottom within a black-stamped panel with a gilt rule boarder. In a board slipcase covered with black paper. White laid paper, all edges trimmed. Endpapers white laid paper. Copies 1 and 2 have dust jackets.

Rare Book Room PS3511.R94 I5 1962a (2 copies)

In the Clearing. Crane A41.1
New York: Holt, Rinehart and Winston, 1962.

First trade edition. Binding: slate-gray medium linen cloth. cream-gray wove stock. Copy 4 inscribed "To Frank Piskor for being and doing so much for me and my tribe. Robert Frost. Cambridge, April 1962."

Rare Book Room PS3511.R94 I5 c.4 (2 copies, numbered 4 and 5)

In the Clearing. Crane A41.2
Introduction by Robert Graves.
London: Holt, Rinehart and Winston, 1962.

First English edition. Binding: slate-gray linen cloth of a slightly coarser texture than the American trade edition. Covers blank. Spine stamped in silver, lettered from top to bottom. White wove paper, all edges trimmed. Endpapers of heavy white "linen-weave" stock. Dust jacket. [7 page typescript of the introduction, heavily corrected in ink and signed on the first page by Graves is located with non-book materials. See page 142.]

Rare Book Room PS3511.R94 I5 1962c

Interviews with Robert Frost.
Edited by Edward Connery Lathem.
New York: Holt, Rinehart and Winston [1966]
First edition. Dust jacket.
Rare Book Room PS3511.R94 I55 1966

Interviews with Robert Frost.
Edited by Edward Connery Lathem.
London: Jonathan Cape, 1967.
[First English edition.] Bound in light tan linen cloth. Spine lettered in gilt on deep purple label. Top edge stained purple. Dust jacket.
Rare Book Room PS3511.R94 I55 1967

Iz Deviati Knig: Perevod s Angliiskogo.
Edited with a foreword by M. A. Zyenkyevich.
Moskva: Izd-vo Inostrannoi Lit-ry, 1963.
Russian translation of *Robert Frost: From Nine Books.* Dust jacket.
Rare Book Room PS3511.R94 A56 1963

Lehtedel Sammuja.
Tallinn: Kirjastus "Eesti Raamat", 1965.
Translation of *Complete Poems of Robert Frost* (N.Y.: Holt, Rinehart and Winston, 1961). Dust jacket.
Rare Book Room PS3511.R94 A53 1965

The Letters of Robert Frost to Louis Untermeyer.
New York: Holt, Rinehart and Winston, c1963.
First edition. Dust jacket.
Rare Book Room PS3511.R94 Z53 c.3

Lider un Poemes.
Translated by Meyer Ziml Tkatch.
New York: [Hoyptfarkoyf: Tsiko], 1965.
Yiddish translation of *Complete Poems of Robert Frost.*
Rare Book Room PS3511.R94 A58 1965

The Lone Striker. C:60
[New York: A.A. Knopf, c1933]

First edition. Binding: buff wrappers with flaps overlapping first and last leaves similar to a dust wrapper but sewn at the spine with a white silk cord knotted on the outside. Drawing by W. A. Dwiggins, printed in black and surrounded by three black rules, occupies almost all of the front cover. Printing on front cover in red. All edges trimmed. Number eight of the Borzoi chap books.

Rare Book Room PS3511.R94 L6 1933

The Lone Striker. New York: Knopf, 1933.
First edition in original wrapper.
Designed by W.A. Dwiggins.

A Masque of Mercy. Crane A31
New York: Henry Holt and Company, c1947.

Edition limited to 751 numbered copies signed by Robert Frost. Copy 1 is number 567 and library's copy 2 is number 76. Binding: beige paper-covered boards backed with dark blue linen cloth. On the front cover in the upper right corner is a black-stamped panel, lettered in gilt stamp within a gilt-stamped rule frame. A vertical gilt rule delineates the juncture between cloth and paper. Spine stamped with gilt within a gilt-ruled black panel reading from bottom to top. Back cover blank with vertical gilt rule delineating the juncture between cloth and paper. In a plain, unlettered slipcase of the same beige paper. White laid paper, all edges trimmed. Endpapers white laid paper.

Rare Book Room PS3511.R94 M26 1947 (2 copies)

[16]

To F.P.P.
I had forgotten I wrote this for Jonathan Cape. I like to hope you will find it interesting play. I weep in parts of it. RF

INTRODUCTION

A ROMANTIC CHASM

HAVING a book in London is not quite the same thing today as it was in 1913 when I had my first book there or anywhere – half a lifetime and two wars ago. To be sure by 1913 I had already had it from Kipling that I was hopelessly hedged from the elder earth with alien speech. But hearing then I heard not. I was young and heedless. My vitality shed discouragement as the well-oiled feathers of a healthy duck shed wetness. And to be merely hedged off was no great matter. What was a hedge to the poacher in my blood of a shiny night in the season of the year? It took an American, a friend, Henry L. Mencken, to rouse me to a sense of national differences. My pedantry would be poor and my desert small with the educated if I could pretend to look unscared into the gulf his great book has made to yawn between the American and English languages.

I wish Edward Thomas (that poet) were here to ponder gulfs in general with me as in the days when he and I tired the sun with talking on the footpaths and stiles of Leddington and Ryton. I should like to ask him if it isn't true that the world is in parts and the separation of the parts as important as the connection of the parts. Isn't the great demand for good spacing? But now I do not know the number of his mansion to write him so much as a letter of inquiry. The mansions so many would probably be numberless. Then I must leave it to Jack Haines in Gloucester to tell me frankly if the gulf in word or idiom has been seriously widening since the night when to illustrate our talk about the internationality of ferns, he boosted me up a small cliff to see by matchlight a spleenwort he knew of there.

5

A Masque of Reason. London: Jonathan Cape, 1948. First English edition. At the head of the introduction, p. 5, Frost has written to Dr. Piskor, "To F.P.P./ I had forgotten I wrote this for Jonathan Cape. I like to hope you find it/ interesting play. I weep in parts/of it./RF." Frost also made corrections in various parts of the book.

A Masque of Mercy. Crane A31.1
New York: Henry Holt and Company, 1947.
First trade edition. Binding: light blue fine linen cloth. Covers blank. Spine gilt-stamped reading from top to bottom. Copies 3 and 4 have dust jackets.
Rare Book Room PS3511.R94 M26 (2 copies, numbered 3 and 4)

A Masque of Reason. Crane A27
New York : Henry Holt and Company, 1945.
Edition limited to 800 numbered copies signed by Robert Frost. Copy 1 is number 594 and library's copy 2 is number 62. Binding: light brown paper-covered boards, backed with tan linen cloth. On the front cover in the upper right corner is a dark brown stamped panel lettered in gilt-stamp. Spine stamped with gilt within a gilt ruled dark brown panel, reading from bottom to top. Back cover blank. In a black board slipcase. White laid paper. Top edge trimmed, fore and bottom edges untrimmed. Endpapers white laid stock.
Rare Book Room PS3511.R94 M3 1945b (2 copies)

A Masque of Reason. Crane A27.1
New York: Henry Holt and Company, 1945.
Trade edition. Binding: dark blue fine linen cloth. Covers blank. Spine stamped in gilt from top to bottom. Rough cream wove paper. Top and bottom edges trimmed, fore edge rough cut. Endpapers of a heavier beige wove paper. Both copies have dust jacket.
Rare Book Room PS3511.R94 M3 1945 (2 copies)

A Masque of Reason. Containing A Masque of Reason: A Masque of Mercy (Two New England Biblicals); together with Steeple Bush and Other Poems. Crane A34
London: Jonathan Cape, 1948.
First English edition. Binding: bright deep blue linen cloth. Covers blank. Spine stamped in silver from bottom to top. Copy 1 is inscribed by the poet with comments on the introduction and corrections in various parts of the book. Note on fly leaf: "See my introduction RF". This copy was in *The Frost 100* travelling exhibit which began at Princeton University Library, May-June 1974. Copies 1 and 2 have dust jackets. Copy 3 is specially bound in leather & tan linen.
Rare Book Room PS3511.R94 M3 1948 (3 copies)

[18] *Mountain Interval.* C:31-32
New York: H. Holt and Company, [c1916]

First edition. Binding: blue cloth; front cover stamped in gilt with double-line rectangle, lettered within. Spine stamped in gilt. Back cover blank. Top edges trimmed, fore and bottom edges untrimmed. Endpapers cream. Copies 1 and 3 are first state, copy 2 is second state. Copy 1 inscribed: "For Frank Piskor/With all its faults to prove it (see/ page 88) to prove it [sic] a very First./ Robert Frost/ in friendship." Copy 2 is gift of William P. Tolley and is inscribed: "Page 12. The trial by market everything must come to. This book didn't take hold. Several own to have owned it. I hereby bring it to rest with Frank Piskor in Friendship. Robert Frost."

MOUNTAIN INTERVAL

BY

ROBERT FROST

Author of "North of Boston"

NEW YORK
HENRY HOLT AND COMPANY

Mountain Interval. New York: Henry Holt, 1916. First edition, first state. Includes the inscription "For Frank Piskor / With all its faults to prove it (see / page 88) to prove it a very First. / Robert Frost / in friendship."

New Hampshire: A Poem with Notes and Grace Notes. C:37-38
Woodcuts by J. J. Lankes.
New York: Henry Holt and Company, 1923.

First edition. Binding: dark green paper-covered boards with a brighter green backstrip. Gilt paper label, sunk in panel on front cover, hand-lettered in black. Spine stamped in gilt. Back cover blank. Top edges trimmed and stained green, fore and bottom edges untrimmed. Endpapers mottled brown. Copies 2 and 3 are first printings, October 1923. Copy 4 is a third printing, May 1924. Copy 2 inscribed by Frost for Earl Bernheimer with the first three lines of "A Star in a Stone-Boat" (p. 21). Dust jacket.

NEW HAMPSHIRE
A POEM WITH NOTES
AND GRACE NOTES BY
ROBERT FROST
WITH WOODCUTS
BY J. J. LANKES
PUBLISHED BY
HENRY HOLT
& COMPANY : NEW
YORK : MCMXXIII

New Hampshire: A Poem With Notes and Grace Notes. New York: Henry Holt, 1923. First edition, first printing.

New Hampshire: A Poem with Notes and Grace Notes. C:39

Woodcuts by J. J. Lankes.

New York: Henry Holt and Company, 1923.

Edition limited to 350 copies signed by author. Library's copy is #193. Binding: black buckram with beveled edges, front cover stamped in upper center with cut in gilt of a grindstone under an apple tree. Spine stamped in gilt. Back cover blank. Top edges trimmed and gilded, fore and bottom edges untrimmed. Endpapers light brown.

Rare Book Room PS3511.R94 N4 1923 c.5

New Hampshire: A Poem with Notes and Grace Notes. Crane A6.1

London: Grant Richards Ltd., 1924.

First English edition. Binding: light gray paper-covered boards. Shelfback of light tan rough linen. Covers blank. Spine lettered in dark blue. Top edge trimmed and stained dull brown, other edges untrimmed. Dust jacket.

Rare Book Room PS3511.R94 N4 1924

New Hampshire, a Poem. Crane A6.2

Hanover, New Hampshire: The New Dresden Press, 1955.

First separate edition. Limited to 750 numbered copies signed by the author. Library's copy is number 316. Binding: gray-brown paper-covered boards, backed with tan crushed linen; the two sections delineated by a thick gilt rule at the juncture. Covers blank. The spine has a gray-brown paper label lettered in gilt vertically from bottom to top. The book has a protective jacket of semitransparent rough white Japanese paper. Top edge trimmed, fore and bottom edges untrimmed. Dust jacket.

Rare Book Room PS3511.R94 N4 1955

North of Boston. C:22-24

London: D. Nutt, 1914.

First edition, first issue. Binding: green buckram; front cover bordered with a blind rule and lettered in gilt. Spine stamped in gilt. Back cover blank. Top edges trimmed, fore and bottom edges untrimmed. Endpapers cream. Inscribed: "To Frank Piskor - My gratitude for several things but particularly for what he has done for one of my young poets. [Philip Booth] This book in this edition takes me back to when I was a young poet (a proud word I never used for myself till others gave it me [sic] as a title. Robert Frost, Cambridge, Mass., April 1962." In brown leather backed slipcase.

Rare Book Room PS3511.R94 N6 1914

North of Boston. C:29-30

New York: Henry Holt and Company, 1915.

Second Edition, 1915 [actually First American edition]. Binding: blue cloth; front cover stamped in gilt with double-line rectangle, lettered within. Spine stamped in gilt. Back cover blank. Top edges trimmed, fore and bottom edges untrimmed. Endpapers cream. Copy 2: "Third edition, 1915." Copy 3: Fourth printing, Dec. 1915. Copy 4: Third printing, Oct. 1915.

Rare Book Room PS3511.R94 N6 1915 (4 copies)

[21]

To Frank Piskor
my gratitude for several things
but particularly for what he has
done for one of my young poets.
This book in this edition takes
me back to when I was a young poet
(a praise word I never used for
myself till others gave it me as
a title

Robert Frost
Cambridge Mass
April 1962

North of Boston. London: David Nutt, 1914. First edition, first issue. Inscribed "To Frank Piskor / My gratitude / for several things / but particularly / for what he has done / for one of my young poets." Refers to Philip Booth, then at Syracuse University with Dr. Piskor.

 North of Boston. C:33

Portrait and illustrations by James Chapin.

New York: Henry Holt and Company, [1919]

Edition limited to 500 copies. This is the first edition with the Chapin illustrations. Binding: gray-green paper-covered boards with darker cloth backstrip. Gilt paper label sunk in panel on front cover, hand-lettered in black. Spine stamped in gilt. Back cover blank. Top edges trimmed, fore and bottom edges untrimmed. Hand-made paper. Endpapers white. From the Library of Hugh Walpole, signed by him in 1933 at the Athenaean Club.

Rare Book Room PS3511.R94 N6 1919

North of Boston: Poems.

Edited by Edward Connery Lathem; woodcuts by J. J. Lankes.

New York: Dodd, Mead, c1977.

Limited edition of 500 copies. Inscribed: "Inscribed for Frank P. Piskor with the warm regard and best wishes of the editor. E. C. Lathem." Dust jacket.

Rare Book Room PS3511.R94 N6 1977

On Emerson.

In *Daedalus: Journal of the American Academy of Arts and Sciences*, vol. 88, no. 4 (Fall 1959), pp. 712-718. An address delivered October 8, 1958 on the occasion of Frost's receipt of the Emerson-Thoreau Medal from the Academy.

Rare Book Room PS3511.R94 O48

One Favored Acorn. Crane A42

[New York: Spiral Press, 1969, c1967]

First separate edition. Limited to 400 copies. Binding: heavy yellow-brown paper wrapper, folded at the fore-edges over the preliminary and terminal blank leaves. Stitched with white thread at the center fold. Lettered on the front cover as above. White laid paper, all edges trimmed. Printed for Middlebury College in celebration of the dedication of the Robert Frost cabin and land in Ripton, Vermont, on July the twelfth, 1969.

Rare Book Room PS3511.R94 O5 1969

The Pocket Book of Robert Frost's Poems.

Introduction by Louis Untermeyer.

New York: Pocket Books, 1946.

First edition, first paperback.

Rare Book Room PS3511.R94 A6 1946

A Pocket Book of Robert Frost's Poems.
Introduction and commentary by Louis Untermeyer;
[illustrated by John O'Hara Cosgrave II.]
New York: Pocket Books, 1956.
Pocket library no. 47. First published in 1943 under title: Come In.
Rare Book Room PS3511.R94 A6 1956

A Pocket Book of Robert Frost's Poems.
New York: Washington Square Press, 1960, c1946.
With an introduction and commentary by Louis Untermeyer. This is an extended version done for Washington Square Press of the original 1943 "Come In" by Louis Untermeyer published by Henry Holt and Company.
Rare Book Room PS3511.R94 A6 1960

Poems by Robert Frost: A Boy's Will and North of Boston.
Introduction by William H. Pritchard.
New York: New American Library;
Markham, Ont.: Penguin Books Canada, c1989 (1990 printing)
Rare Book Room PS3511.R94 B6 1989

The Poems of Robert Frost Crane A29
New York: Modern Library, [1946]
First edition of this selection. Binding: blue-gray very fine linen cloth. Front cover with a single gilt rule frame around a black cloth panel bordered with gilt rule, lettered in gilt. Modern Library device gilt stamped in lower right corner of frame. Spine gilt stamped, back cover blank. White wove paper, all edges trimmed. Top edge stained dark green. Endpapers of wove paper printed on the facing paste-down and open endpaper recto with the Modern Library devices in gray and white. Contains first printing of "The Constant Symbol." Dust jacket.
Rare Book Room PS3511 .R94 1946

The Poetry of Robert Frost.
Edited by Edward Connery Lathem.
Barre, Mass.: Imprint Society, 1971.
Limited to 1950 copies. Library's copy is number 1516.
Two volumes in slipcase.
Rare Book Room PS3511.R94 1971 v.1 and 2

[24] *The Prophets Really Prophesy as Mystics the Commentators Merely by Statistics.*
In *Poetry: The Fiftieth Anniversary.* vol. 101, nos. 1/2 (October/November 1962), pp. 41-42.
Rare Book Room PS3511.R94 P76 1962

Prose Jottings of Robert Frost:
Selections from His Notebooks and Miscellaneous Manuscripts.
Edited by Edward Connery Lathem and Hyde Cox;
with an introduction by Kathleen Johnston Morrison.
Lunenburg, Vt.: Northeast-Kingdom Publishers, c1982.
First edition, limited to 1600 copies. Design, letter press, and binding by The Stinehour Press.
Rare Book Room PS3511.R94 A6 1982b

Robert Frost.
Edited and with an introduction by Geoffrey Moore.
New York: Clarkson N. Potter, Inc.; Distributed by Crown
Publishers, c1986.
First edition. Dust jacket.
Rare Book Room PS3511.R94 A6 1986

Robert Frost.
Edited by Roger Asselineau.
[Paris]: Pierre Seghers, c1964.
Limited to 8 copies on Holland paper. Library's copy is letter E. Library's copy is hand bound. Poetes d'aujourd'hui: 122.
Rare Book Room PS3511.R94 Z519 1964

Robert Frost, a Tribute to the Source.
New York: Holt, Rinehart and Winston, c1979.
First edition.
Rare Book Room PS3511.R94 Z518 1979

Robert Frost: Farm-poultryman: The Story of Robert Frost's Career as a Breeder and Fancier of Hens & the Texts of Eleven Long-forgotten Prose Contributions by the Poet, Which Appeared in Two New England Poultry Journals in 1903-05, During His Years of Farming at Derry, New Hampshire.
Edited by Edward Connery Lathem & Lawrance Thompson.

Hanover, N. H.: Dartmouth Publications, 1963.

Dust jacket.

Rare Book Room PS3511.R94 A16 1963

Robert Frost on "Extravagance": The Text of Robert Frost's Last College Lecture, Delivered at Dartmouth College on the Evening of November 27, 1962.

[s.l. : s.n., 1963?]

Reprinted from the Dartmouth alumni magazine of March 1963.

Rare Book Room PS3511.R94 R58 1963

Robert Frost: Poetry and Prose.

Edited by Edward Connery Lathem and Lawrance Thompson.

New York: Holt, Rinehart and Winston, c1972.

Rinehart editions, 154.

Rare Book Room PS3511.R94 A6 1972 c.2

Robert Frost: Toward the Source, Against the Stream.

[New York: A. Colish, Inc., 1990]

Limited to 350 copies. Poems published for a special benefit performance by the Writers in performance at the Manhattan Theatre Club.

Rare Book Room PS3511.R94 R6 1990

Seasons.

Poems selected by Edward Connery Lathem with photographs by Christopher Burkett.

New York: Henry Holt and Company, 1992.

First edition. Dust jacket.

Rare Book Room PS3511.R94 S38 1992

Selected Letters.

Edited by Lawrance Thompson.

New York: Holt, Rinehart and Winston, c1964.

First edition. Copy 2 has inscription by editor on half-title page to Frank Piskor.

Rare Book Room PS3511.R94 Z52 1964 c.2

[26] *Selected Poems.* C:34-35

New York: Henry Holt and Company, 1923.

First edition. Binding: gray paper-covered boards decorated with a recurring wreath design in gilt. Backstrap of dark green cloth, stamped in gilt. Front and back covers blank. Top edges trimmed and stained green, fore and bottom edges untrimmed. Endpapers cream. Copy 1 was Arthur Davison Fiche's copy and is signed by him. Copy 2 has dust jacket and is a later printing, December, 1924.

Rare Book Room PS3511.R94 A6 1923 (2 copies)

Selected Poems. C:36

London: W. Heinemann; New York: H. Holt and Co., 1923.

First English edition. Binding: dark blue cloth, front and back covers blank, white paper label on spine printed in red. Top edges trimmed, fore and bottom edges untrimmed. Endpapers white. Dust jacket.

Rare Book Room PS3511.R94 A6 1923b

Selected Poems. C:46-47

New York: Henry Holt and Company [c1928]

Revised edition. First edition of expanded collection. Binding: gray paper-covered boards with green cloth backstrip. Front cover stamped in gilt with facsimile of Frost's autograph in lower right corner. Spine stamped in gilt. Back cover blank. All edges trimmed, top edge stained green. Endpapers white. Copy 1 has dust jacket.

Rare Book Room PS3511.R94 A6 1928 (2 copies)

Selected Poems. C:64-65

New York: Henry Holt and Company [c1934]

Third edition. Binding: pale blue buckram. Autograph stamped in gilt in lower righthand corner of front cover. Spine stamped in gilt. Back cover blank. All edges trimmed. End-papers blue. Inscribed: "Dear Frank: 'Bereft,' p. 21. I read at the graveside of a dear friend, Ethel Stewart, the widow of my old Comparative Literature professor, W. K. Stewart. It proved quite moving. Herbert West." Dust jacket.

Rare Book Room PS3511.R94 A6 1934

Selected Poems. C:77-79

Chosen by the author; with introductory essays by W.H. Auden, C. Day Lewis, Paul Engle and Edwin Muir.

London: Jonathan Cape, [1936]

First edition. Binding: blue linen. Front and back covers blank. Spine lettered in gilt. Top edges trimmed and stained blue; fore edges trimmed; bottom edges untrimmed. Endpapers white. Dust jacket.

Rare Book Room PS3511.R94 A6 1936

Selected Poems. Crane A38

Introduction by C. Day Lewis.

Harmondsworth [England]: Penguin Books, 1955.

First edition of this selection. Binding: heavy wove paper wrappers with an overall pattern of two stylized black ornaments arranged alternately in rows against a ground of light tan dotted with white. On front cover is a white panel with a triple thin-thick-thin rule inside the border, lettered in black. Spine lettered in black with rules in tan on a panel of white. Back cover without lettering. Cream wove paper, all edges trimmed, cover cut flush with leaves.

Rare Book Room PS3511.R94 A6 1955 (3 copies)

Selected Poems.

New York: Gramercy Books: Distributed by Outlet Book Co., c1992.

Dust jacket.

Rare Book Room PS3511.R94 A6 1992

Selected Poems of Robert Frost.

Introduction by Robert Graves.

New York: Holt, Rinehart and Winston, 1963.

First edition. Paperback. Frost made several minor changes in the texts of several poems in this selection.

Rare Book Room PS3511.R94 A6 1963

Selected Poems of Robert Frost.

Translated into Persian by F. Mojtabai.

Tehran: Sokhan Publications, 1960.

New World Poetry Series: Bilingual edition.

Rare Book Room PS3511.R94 A17 1960

Selected Prose of Robert Frost.

Edited by Hyde Cox and Edward Connery Lathem.

New York: Holt, Rinehart and Winston, c1966.

First edition. Both library copies have dust jackets.

Rare Book Room PS3511.R94 A16 1966 (2 copies)

[28] *Selected Prose of Robert Frost.*
Edited by Hyde Cox and Edward Connery Lathem.
New York: Collier Books, [1968, c1966]
First Collier Books edition.

A Sermon. Crane A33
Cincinnati: Victor E. Reichert, 1947.
First edition. Limited edition of 500 copies printed for Dr. Reichert at the Spiral Press. Binding: gray-red wove paper wrappers cut flush with the leaves and folded over pp. 1-2 and 19-20. A gray paper label is pasted in a slightly larger blind-stamped panel on the front cover. Stapled at center fold. Cream laid paper, all edges trimmed. Delivered on the first day of the feast of Tabernacles, at the Rockdale Avenue Temple, Cincinnati, Ohio, Thursday morning, October 10, 1946. Copy 1 is one of the 500; copy 2 is a photocopy.

A SERMON BY Robert Frost

SPOKEN ON THE FIRST DAY OF

THE FEAST OF TABERNACLES AT

THE ROCKDALE AVENUE TEMPLE

CINCINNATI · OHIO · THURSDAY

MORNING · OCTOBER · 10 · 1946

A Sermon. New York: Spiral Press, 1947. 1/500 copies with a cover letter from Joseph Blumenthal forwarding it to Frank Piskor as a gift. One of the few times Frost spoke on the subject of religion.

Several Short Poems. C:41
Woodcut by J. J. Lankes.
New York: H. Holt, [1924]

Only edition. Limited to 2000 copies. This is a single sheet of grayish handmade paper folded once to make four pages. Copy 2 inscribed by Frost "To Russell from RF". [Russell was an early recipient of materials from Frost who later had a falling out over his selling these gifts.]

Rare Book Room PS3511.R94 A6 1924 (2 copies)

Steeple Bush. Crane A30
New York: Henry Holt and Company, 1947.

Edition limited to 751 numbered copies signed by Robert Frost. Copy 1 is number 323 and library's copy 2 is number 57. Binding: gray-green paper-covered boards backed with tan linen cloth. On front cover is Loren MacIver's title-page design repeated in gilt-stamp. Spine stamped in gilt within a gilt ruled black panel, lettered from bottom to top. Back cover blank. In a plain, unlettered slipcase covered with gray-green paper used for the binding. White wove paper. Top and bottom edges trimmed, fore edge untrimmed. Endpapers white wove paper.

Rare Book Room PS3511.R94 S7 1947b (2 copies)

SEVERAL
SHORT POEMS

By

ROBERT FROST

Woodcut — By J. J. Lankes

THE PASTURE

I'M going out to clean the pasture spring;
I'll only stop to rake the leaves away
(And wait to watch the water clear, I may):
I shan't be gone long.—You come too.

I'm going out to fetch the little calf
That's standing by the mother. It's so young,
It totters when she licks it with her tongue.
I shan't be gone long.—You come too.

Copyright by Henry Holt and Company

Several Short Poems, New York: Henry Holt, 1924. One sheet folded. Inscribed by Frost "For Russell from RF." Russell was an early recipient of material from Frost who later had a falling out with the poet over his selling these gifts. Limited to 2,000 copies "but much scarcer than that number would indicate" (Appraiser).

[30] *Steeple Bush.* Crane A30.1

New York: Henry Holt and Company, [1947]

First trade edition. Binding: light blue-green fine linen cloth. Cover blank. Spine lettered in gilt from top to bottom within a gilt-ruled black panel. White laid paper, all edges trimmed. Endpapers of heavier white wove paper. Copy 3 has dust jacket and is a second printing, June, 1947.

Rare Book Room PS3511.R94 S7 1947 (2 copies, numbered 2 and 3)

Stopping by Woods on a Snowy Evening.

Illustrated by Susan Jeffers.

New York: Dutton, [1978]

First edition.

Rare Book Room PS3511.R94 S76

Stories for Lesley.

Illustrated by Warren Chappell; edited by Roger D. Sell.

[Charlottesville, VA]: Published for the Bibliographical Society of the University of Virginia by the University Press of Virginia, c1984.

Eighteen stories written by Robert Frost for his children on their New England farm between the years 1899 and 1907 or 1908. Dust jacket.

Rare Book Room PS3511.R94 S78 1984

A Talk for Students: Crane D14

An Extemporaneous Talk at the Twenty-eighth Annual Commencement of Sarah Lawrence College, Bronxville, New York, June 7, 1956.

New York: Distributed by The Fund for the Republic, [1956?]

Rare Book Room PS3511.R94 T34 1956 (2 copies)

Three Poems. C:66

Hanover, N.H.: Baker Library Press, [c1935]

First edition. Limited to 125 copies. Library's copy is number 37. Binding: light blue paper wrappers, sewn. White label on front cover lettered in black. Bordered by double rules in blue, outside rule heavier than inside. Back cover blank. Six sheets sewn with light blue silk. Top edges trimmed, fore and bottom edges untrimmed. No endpapers.

Rare Book Room PS3511.R94 A17 1935

The Message the Crow Gave me for Lesley one Morning Lately when I went to the Well

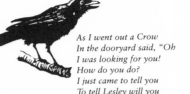

As I went out a Crow
In the dooryard said, "Oh
I was looking for you!
How do you do?
I just came to tell you
To tell Lesley will you
That her little Bluebird
Wanted me to bring word
That the north wind last night
That made the stars bright
And made ice on the trough
Almost made him cough
His tail feathers off.
He just had to fly
But he sent her Goodbye
And said to be good
And wear her red hood
And look for skunk tracks
In the snow with an axe
And do everything
And perhaps in the spring
He would come back and sing."

ROBERT FROST

Stories for Lesley

Illustrated by Warren Chappell

Edited by Roger D. Sell

Published for the
Bibliographical Society of the University of Virginia
by the UNIVERSITY PRESS OF VIRGINIA

Stories for Lesley. Charlottesville, VA: Published for the Bibliographical Society of the University of Virginia by the University Press of Virginia, 1984. Written for Frost's children between 1899 and 1907 or 1908.

 An Uncompleted Revision of Education by Poetry, Published in Facsimile As a Keepsake of a Robert Frost Gathering Held at Dartmouth College, Baker Memorial Library on July 3, 1966.
[n.p., 1966]
Original title page reads: Amherst Alumni Council news. Education by poetry, a meditative monologue, by Robert Frost. Supplement to [volume] IV, number 4 [March] 1931. Reproduced from the mutilated Dartmouth College copy, with mss. revisions by the author. First published in the Amherst graduates' quarterly, Feb. 1913.
Rare Book Room PS3511.R94 E3 1966 (2 copies)

A Way Out: A One Act Play. C:48
New York: Harbor Press, 1929.
Limited edition. 485 copies printed at the Harbour Press. Library's copy is number 278. Binding: salmon-colored paper-covered boards with black cloth backstrip. On each vertical edge of the backstrip where it overlaps the front and back covers there are stamped in gilt two wavy lines. Front and back covers otherwise blank. Spine lettered in gilt from bottom to top. All edges untrimmed. Endpapers white. Signed by Frost. In custom-made slipcase. Included in AIGA 50 Best Books of the Year.
Rare Book Room PS3511.R94 W39 1929

West-running Brook. C:44-45
Woodcuts by J. J. Lankes.
New York: H. Holt, [c1928]
Edition limited to 1000 numbered copies signed by the author. Library's copy is number 133. Binding: gray paper-covered boards decorated with falling leaves in autumn colors; green cloth backstrip. Front and back cover blank. Spine stamped in gilt from bottom to top. Top edges trimmed and gilded; fore and bottom edges untrimmed. Endpapers white matching sheets. Last line on p. 38 reads "rooms" instead of "romps." Included in AIGA 50 Best Books of the year.
Rare Book Room PS3511.R94 W4 1928

WEST-RUNNING
BROOK

BY

ROBERT FROST

NEW YORK
HENRY HOLT AND COMPANY

West-running Brook. New York: Henry Holt, 1928. First edition. Inscribed by Frost to Frank Piskor with the poem “Once by the Pacific” copied by Frost.

[34] *West-running Brook.* C:42-43

New York, Henry Holt and Company, [1928]

First edition. Binding: green paper-covered boards with a green cloth backstrip. Gilt paper label sunk in panel on front cover bearing a reproduction in miniature of the frontispiece to the book. Spine lettered from bottom to top. Back cover blank. Top edges trimmed and stained green, fore and bottom edges untrimmed. Endpapers mottled brown. 9,400 copies of the First edition were printed, but it is generally believed that of those only 1,000 copies contained the words "First Edition" on the verso of the title page. Dust jacket contains first printings of "Some Definitions" [of Poetry]. Copy 1 first state and is inscribed by Frost to Frank Piskor with the poem "Once by the Pacific" copied by Frost. Only one of the library's copies to contain the words "First Edition." Copy 3 signed by Frost. Copies 1 and 3 have dust jackets.

Rare Book Room PS3511.R94 W4 1928a (6 copies, numbered 1, 3-7)

West-running Brook.

New York: Holt, c1928, [1935]

Later edition, March 1935. Binding: green paper-covered boards with a green cloth backstrip. Gilt paper label sunk in panel on front cover bearing a reproduction in miniature of the frontispiece to the book. Spine lettered from bottom to top. Back cover blank. In this printing, the second word of the last line on p. 44 has been altered to "romps" from the first-printing "roams." Inscribed to Frank Piskor, "Robert Frost B.L. 1936". Frost again inscribed the book on his visit to Syracuse University: "Revalidated at Syracuse University April 21, 1959 after a great ride from Amherst College talking all the way." Dust jacket.

Rare Book Room PS3511.R94 W4 1935

Robert Frost
B.L. 1936
revalidated at
Syracuse University
April 21 1959
after a great ride
from Amherst College
talking all the way

WEST-RUNNING BROOK

West-running Brook. New York: Henry Holt, 1935. Inscribed to Frank Piskor, Bread Loaf, VT. "Robert Frost B.L. 1936." Frost inscribed the book again on a later visit to Syracuse University, after Dr. Piskor had chauffeured the poet from Amherst to Syracuse: "Revalidated at Syracuse University April 21, 1959 after a great ride from Amherst College talking all the way."

[36] *A Witness Tree.* Crane A25

New York: Henry Holt & Company, 1942.

Edition limited to 735 numbered copies signed by Robert Frost. Copy 1 is number 421 and library's copy 2 is number 256. Binding: gray-green decorative paper-covered boards with an overall design of leaves, dots, and dashes. Dark gray-green linen cloth backstrip. A gilt rule runs vertically delineating the juncture between the cloth and paper. Spine stamped in gilt with lettering from bottom to top. Back cover unlettered. Cream laid paper. Top edge trimmed, fore-edge uncut, bottom edge rough cut. Endpapers of the same stock. Both copies in slipcase. Included in AIGA 50 Best Books of the Year.

Rare Book Room PS3511.R94 W5 1942a (2 copies)

A Witness Tree. Crane A25.1

New York: Henry Holt and Company, [1942]

First trade edition. Binding: greenish blue linen cloth. Front cover stamped in gilt, spine gilt stamped and lettered from top to bottom. Back cover blank. White wove fibrous paper. Top edge trimmed and stained dark green, fore edge uncut, bottom edge rough cut. Endpapers of heavy wove light orange-yellow paper. Copy 2 is later printing, June, 1942. Copy 3 is later printing, March 1943.

Rare Book Room PS3511.R94 W5 (2 copies, numbered 2 and 3)

A Witness Tree. Crane A25.2

London: Jonathan Cape, [1943]

First English edition. Binding: blue linen cloth. Covers blank; spine lettered in gilt from top to bottom. Dust jacket.

Rare Book Room PS3511.R94 W5 1943

You Come Too: Favourite Poems for Young Readers.

Selected and edited by Robert Frost; foreword by Eleanor Farjeon; illustrated by Cecile Curtis.

London: Bodley Head, 1964.

First English edition. Dust jacket.

Rare Book Room PS3511.R94 Y6 1964

WORKS WITH CONTRIBUTIONS BY FROST

Adams, Frederick B., Jr. Ewert:60
To Russia with Frost.
Engravings by Thomas W. Nason.
Boston: Club of Odd Volumes, 1963.
First edition, limited. "The edition of this book consists of five hundred copies designed by Joseph Blumenthal and printed at The Spiral Press, New York."
Rare Book Room PS3511.R94 Z54 1963

The American Mercury Reader; a Selection of Distinguished Articles, Stories, and Poems Published in "The American Mercury" During the Past Twenty Years.
Edited by Lawrence E. Spivak and Charles Angoff.
Philadelphia: The Blakiston Company, 1944.
Includes poem, "A Leaf-treader," by Robert Frost on p. 338.
Rare Book Room PS536 .A56 1944 c.2

American Poetry, 1922: A Miscellany.
New York: Harcourt, Brace and Company, 1922.
Includes five poems by Robert Frost pp. 25-38. Dust jacket.
Rare Book Room PS614 .A6712

American Poetry 1927: A Miscellany.
New York: Harcourt, Brace and Company, c1927.
"First edition, August 1927." Includes poems by Robert Frost, "Sand Dunes," "The Flower Boat," "The Birthplace," "The Passing Glimpse," and "Lodged."
Rare Book Room PS3511.R94 A6 1927

Amerikanskie Poety.
Moskva: Khudozh Lit-ra, 1969.
Russian translations of some of Robert Frost's poetry on pp. 127-135. Perevodakh M. Zenkevicha. Dust jacket.
Rare Book Room PS619.R8 A64 1969

An Annual of New Poetry, 1917.
London: Constable and Company Ltd., 1917.
Includes six poems by Robert Frost pp. 63-71.
Rare Book Room PR1225 .A6 (2 copies)

Anthology of Magazine Verse for 1916: And Year Book of American Poetry.
Edited by William Stanley Braithwaite.
New York: Lawrence J. Gomme, 1916.
Second edition. Includes the poem "In the Home Stretch" by Robert Frost on pp. 90-97.
Rare Book Room PS614.A678 1916a

Anthology of Magazine Verse for 1958 and Anthology of Poems from the Seventeen Previously Published Braithwaite Anthologies.
Edited by William Stanley Braithwaite and Margaret Haley Carpenter.
New York: The Schulte Publishing Company, 1959.
Include 6 poems by Robert Frost on pp. 69-83 and pp. 285-290. Dust jacket.
Rare Book Room PS614 .A678 1959

The Arts Anthology: Dartmouth Verse, 1925.
Introduction by Robert Frost; pp. vii-ix.
Portland, Maine: The Mosher Press, 1925.
First edition. Limited to 500 numbered copies. Copy 1 is number 208 and library's copy 2 is number 244.
Rare Book Room PN6110.C7 A7 1925 (2 copies)

Barry, Elaine.
Robert Frost On Writing.
New Brunswick, N.J.: Rutgers University Press, c1973.
Dust jacket.
Rare Book Room PS3511.R94 Z52 1973 c.2

Benet, William Rose, editor.
Fifty Poets: An American Auto-Anthology.
New York City: Duffield and Green, c1933.
Includes poem "Birches" by Robert Frost on pp. 30-31.
Rare Book Room PS614 .B45

Boggs, Tom, editor.
American Decade; 68 Poems for the First Time in an Anthology.
[Cummington, MA.]: The Cummington Press, c1943.

Includes the poem "A Serious Step Lightly Taken" by Robert Frost. Limited to 475 copies, of which fifty are not for sale. Designed and published by the Cummington Press, Cummington, Massachusetts. Dust jacket.

Rare Book Room PS614 .B513

The Book of Noble Thoughts.
Edited by Louis Untermeyer; illustrated by Rockwell Kent.
New York: American Artists Group, 1946.

Includes excerpt from poem, "The Death of the Hired Man" by Robert Frost on page 113. Copy 1 has dust jacket.

Rare Book Room PN6331 .U5 1946 (2 copies)

A Book of Poems for Every Mood.
Edited by Harriet Monroe and Morton Dauwen Zabel.
Illustrated by Janet Laura Scott.
Racine, WI: Whitman Publishing Co., c1933.

Includes poems by Robert Frost, "The Cow in Apple-time," "Tree at My Window," and " Acquainted with the Night."

Rare Book Room PS586 .B66 1933

A Book of Yale Review Verse.
Foreword by the editors.
New Haven: Yale University Press; London: Humphrey Milford, Oxford University Press, 1917.

Includes a poem by Robert Frost, "The Hill Wife," on pp. [14]-17.

Rare Book Room PN6110.C7 .Y34 1917

The Bookman Anthology of Verse. Second Series.
Edited by John Farrar.
New York: George H. Doran Company, c1927.

Includes a selection on Robert Frost and the poem, "A Fountain, a Bottle, a Donkey's Ears, and Some Books" on pp. 23-29.

Rare Book Room PS614 .B6 1927

 Bread Loaf Anthology.
Introduction and preface by Robert Frost.
Middlebury, VT: Middlebury College Press, 1939.
"Work contributed by Bread Loaf English students and staff, members of the Writers' conference, and alumni and faculty of Middlebury college."
Rare Book Room PS614 .B77 (3 copies)

Burnett, Whit, editor.
America's 93 Greatest Living Authors Present This is My Best: Over 150 Self-chosen and Complete Masterpieces, Together With Their Reasons for Their Selections.
New York: Dial Press, 1942.
Includes sixteen poems and commentary by Robert Frost pp. 277-292.
Rare Book Room PS536 .B8 (2 copies)

Burnett, Whit, editor.
105 Greatest Living Authors Present The World's Best: Stories, Humor, Drama, Biography, History, Essays, Poetry.
New York: Dial Press, 1950.
Includes six poems and commentary by Robert Frost pp. 52-60. Dust jacket.
Rare Book Room PN6014 .B8

Burroughs, Stephen.
Memoirs of the Notorious Stephen Burroughs of New Hampshire.
Preface by Robert Frost.
New York: Lincoln MacVeagh, Dial Press, 1924.
"Reprinted from the Albany edition of 1811."
Rare Book Room CT275.B8 A3 1924

A Catalogue of the Imagist Poets, With Essays.
Essays by Wallace Martin and Ian Fletcher.
New York: J. Howard Woolmer, 1966.
Includes the poem, "Poets Are Born Not Made" by Robert Frost on pp. 36-37.
Rare Book Room PS310.I5 C38

Cleghorn, Sarah Norcliffe.
Threescore: The Autobiography of Sarah N. Cleghorn.
Introduction by Robert Frost.

New York: Harrison Smith & Robert Haas, 1936.
First printing. Copy 1 is signed by the author.
Rare Book Room PS3505.L58 Z5 1936 (2 copies)

Come Christmas: A Selection of Christmas Poetry, Song, Drama and Prose.
Edited by Lesley Frost.
New York: Coward-McCann, Inc., c1935.
Includes facsimile of Robert Frost manuscript "Good Relief" on preliminary pages. Includes "Good Relief" (p. 4) and "Christmas Trees" (pp. 56-8) by Robert Frost. Copy 1 has dust jacket. Copy 2 is inscribed to Frank Piskor by Lesley Frost.
Rare Book Room PS3511.R924 C6 1935 (2 copies)

Congresso Internacional de Escritores e Encontros Intelectuais (1st ed.: 1954: Sao Paulo, Brazil)
Congresso Internacional de Escritores e Encontros Intelectuais.
Sao Paulo: Anhembi, 1957.
Spanish edition. At head of title: Sociedade paulista de escritores. Includes a response by Robert Frost on pp. 459-461.
Rare Book Room PN33 .C66 1954

Cook, Reginald Lansing.
Robert Frost, a Living Voice.
Amherst: University of Massachusetts Press, 1974.
Includes transcripts of twelve talks by Frost, originally delivered at the Bread Loaf School of English, Middlebury College during the last decade of his life. Copy 2 includes presentation by author and accompanying letter from the author. Copies 2 and 3 have dust jackets.
Rare Book Room PS3511.R94 Z586 (2 copies)

Cox, Sidney.
A Swinger of Birches; a Portrait of Robert Frost.
Introduction by Robert Frost.
New York: New York University Press, 1957.
Dust jacket.
Rare Book Room PS3511.R94 Z59 c.2

Doyle, John Robert, Jr.
Sources of "West-running Brook": In Memory of Robert Frost on the Centennial of His Birth.
Charleston, SC: The Citadel, 1974.
Includes excerpts from Frost's poetry. The Citadel: Monograph Series: Number XIII.
Rare Book Room PS3511.R94 W43 1974

Dunbar, Olivia Howard.
A House in Chicago.
Chicago, IL: University of Chicago Press, c1947.
Contains numerous references to Robert Frost and letters written by Frost to Harriet C. Moody.
Rare Book Room CT275.M5846 D8

Engle, Paul and Langland, Joseph, eds.
Poet's Choice.
New York: Dial Press, 1962.
Includes the poem, "Choose Something Like a Star," and commentary by Robert Frost on pp. 1-2. Dust jacket.
Rare Book Room PS614 .E57

Flanders, Helen Hartness and Olney, Marguerite.
Ballads Migrant in New England.
Introduction by Robert Frost.
New York: Farrar, Straus and Young, c1953.
Most of the ballads with music (unaccompanied melodies). Dust jacket.
Rare Book Room M1629.F58 B3

Fox, Frederic.
14 Africans vs. One American.
Introduction by Robert Frost and the author.
New York: Macmillan Company, c1962.
First printing. Dust jacket.
Rare Book Room LA1501 .F6

Francis, Robert.
Frost: A Time to Talk; Conversations & Indiscretions Recorded by Robert Francis.
[Amherst]: University of Massachusetts Press, c1972.
Dust jacket.
Rare Book Room PS3511.R94 Z653 c.2

Francis, Robert.
Robert Frost, A Time to Talk: Conversations & Indiscretions.
London: Robson Books, 1973.
Originally published: Amherst: University of Massachusetts Press, 1972.
Library's copy includes a dedication to Andrew Peters, signed by the author.
Dust jacket.
Rare Book Room PS3511.R94 Z653 1973

A Friendly Visit: Poems for Robert Frost.
Illustrated by John McNee.
Beloit, WI: Beloit College, 1957.
Chapbook Number Five.
Rare Book Room PS3511.R94 Z48 1957

Frost, Lesley.
New Hampshire's Child; the Derry Journals of Lesley Frost.
Notes and index by Lawrence Thompson and Arnold Grade.
Albany, NY: State University of New York Press, 1969.
Includes seven poems by Robert Frost. Copy 2 has inscription to Frank Piskor by the author. Dust jacket.
Rare Book Room PS3511.R924 Z655 c.2

The Future of Man, a Symposium Sponsored by Joseph E. Seagram & Sons, Inc. on the Dedication of Its Headquarters Building in New York at 375 Park Avenue.
[New York?, 1959]
Includes a statement by Robert Frost on pp. 15-17. Frost's participation in the panel discussion begins on p. 48. Library's copy is a xerox copy contained in a hardcover portfolio.
Rare Book Room GN4 .F87 1959

In Other Words; Amherst in Prose and Verse.
Edited by Horace W. Hewlett.
Amherst, MA: Amherst College Press, 1964.
Includes 2 selections by Robert Frost on pp. 159-184.
Rare Book Room LD156 .I5 1964

Lathem, Edward Connery, editor.
A Concordance to the Poetry of Robert Frost.
New York: Holt Information Systems, c1971.
Based on the text of "The Poetry of Robert Frost" (New York: Holt, Rinehart and Winston, 1969)."
Rare Book Room PS3511.R94 Z49 1971

Middlebury College.
Robert Frost, A Tribute From Middlebury College.
Middlebury, VT: Middlebury College Press, [1963]
Includes quotations from "Reluctance" by Robert Frost. Tributes by: Samuel S. Stratton, Egbert C. Hadley, William Hazlett Upson, Ann Wadsworth, and professor Reginald Cook. Portrait of Robert Frost by Gardner Cox.
Rare Book Room PS3511.R94 Z789 1963 (3 copies)

Miscellany: A Co-operative Venture in Wartime Printing.
Typography by Ray Nash. Wood engraving by J. J. Lankes.
Boston: Society of Printers, 1945.
Includes a prose article by Robert Frost, "The Four Beliefs."
Rare Book Room Z120 .M57 1945

New Hampshire Federation of Women's Clubs.
An Anthology of New Hampshire Poetry.
Compiled and edited by The Committee,
Edith Haskell Tappan, Chairman.
Manchester, NH: New Hampshire Federation of Women's Clubs, c1938.
Includes "Robert Frost and New Hampshire" by Robert S. Newdick, pp. 3-6, and six poems by Robert Frost, pp. 7-16.
Rare Book Room PS548.N4 N4 (2 copies)

New Poets of England and America.
Edited by Donald Hall, Robert Pack and Louis Simpson; introduction by Robert Frost.
New York: Meridian Books, Inc., c1957.
Dust jacket.
Rare Book Room PS614 .N48 1957 (2 copies)

The Old Farmers Almanac (Dublin, NH) no. 150 (1942), p. 2
"Rich in Stones" located on p. 2. Its first printing was in this issue of *The Old Farmer's Almanack.* Twelve other poems "on the calendar pages have been chosen by Robert Frost from his *Collected Works* published by Henry Holt & Co. of New York." p. 2
Rare Book Room PS3511.R94 R44

Pearce, Roy Harvey.
The Continuity of American Poetry.
Princeton, NJ: Princeton University Press, 1961.
Includes commentary on and poems by Robert Frost.
Dust jacket.
Rare Book Room PS303 .P4 c.2

The Poetry Quartos: Twelve Brochures, Each Containing a New Poem by an American Poet.
Designed and printed by Paul Johnston.
New York: Random House, 1929.
"475 copies printed in Silvermine Connecticut ..." Includes the first edition of the poem, "The Lovely Shall Be Choosers," by Robert Frost.
Rare Book Room PS614.P64 1929

Prize Poems, 1913-1929.
Edited by Charles A. Wagner, with an introduction by Mark Van Doren.
[New York]: Albert & Charles Boni, 1936.
The winning poems in contests conducted by *Poetry*, *The Dial*, *The Nation* and other periodicals, 1913-1929. Includes poem "The Witch of Coos" by Robert Frost on pp. 85-91. Dust jacket.
Rare Book Room PS614 .P7 1936

[46] *Rabindranath Tagore, 1861-1961: A Centenary Volume.*
New Delhi: Sahitya Akademi, 1961.
Includes a statement by Robert Frost on p. 298.
Rare Book Room PK1718.T24 Z89 1961

Rand, Frank Prentice.
Heart O' Town.
Amherst, MA: Privately Printed, 1945.
Library's copy is signed by the author. Dust jacket.
Rare Book Room PS3535.A552 H4

Reichert, Victor E.
Tower of David, 1964.
Middlebury, VT: Vermont Books, 1964.
"The couplet on page 12 spoken by Mr. Frost is his poem "Forgive, O Lord" from *In the Clearing*, by Robert Frost". Dust jacket.
Rare Book Room PS3535.E395 T6 1964

Richards, Mrs. Waldo [Gertrude Moore], compiler.
High Tide; Songs of Joy and Vision From the Present-Day Poets of America and Great Britain.
Boston, New York: Houghton Mifflin Company, c1916.
Includes two poems by Robert Frost on p. 65 and p. 85.
Rare Book Room PR1225 .R5 1916

Robert Frost and Bread Loaf.
Middlebury, VT: Middlebury College Press, 1964.
Limited edition. Contains correspondence from Robert Frost, an address by Reginald L. Cook, director of the Bread Loaf School of English, delivered June 26, 1963, and addresses delivered at the "Memorial evening" held by the School of English in honor of Robert Frost, July 11, 1963, in the Bread Loaf Theatre.
Rare Book Room PS3511.R94 Z916 1964 (5 copies)

Robert Frost, Great American Poet; From the Wisdom of Robert Frost.
[S.l.: s.n.], 1962.
Hardbound magazine. Contains section on Frost.
Rare Book Room PS3511.R94 Z9162

Robert Frost, His 'American Send-off' - 1915.
Edited by Edward Connery Lathem.
Lunenberg, VT: The Stinehour Press, c1963.
Limited to 325 copies issued in February 1963. Copy 1 is inscribed by Edward Connery Lathem.
Rare Book Room PS3511.R94 Z9161 1963 (2 copies)

Robert Frost i Inni Amerykanscy Poeci: Tlumaczenia.
[London: Poets' & Painters' Press.], 1970.
Slavic edition. At head of title: Aleksander Janta.
Rare Book Room PS619.P6 R62 1970

Robinson, Edwin Arlington. Hogan:46-47
King Jasper; A Poem by Edwin Arlington Robinson.
Introduction by Robert Frost.
New York: The Macmillan Company, 1935.
First edition limited to 250 numbered copies. Library's copy is number 100. Binding: green cloth with black cloth backstrap. Stamped in gold on front cover is facsimile of author's signature. Spine stamped in gold. Top edge gilt, fore and bottom edges untrimmed. Inscribed: "In 1934 Robert Frost to Russell Alberts" on p. xv.
Rare Book Room PS3535.O25 K5 1935

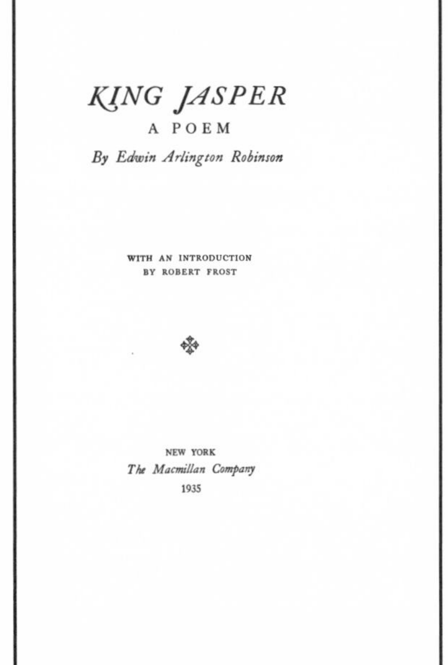

Robinson, Edwin Arlington. *King Jasper*. New York: Macmillan, 1935. 100/150. Introduction by Frost. [Dr. Piskor gave his Edwin Arlington Robinson collection to St. Lawrence University in 1980.]

Ryan, Alvan S.
"Frost and Emerson: Voice and Vision."
The Massachusetts Review: Quarterly of Literature, the Arts and Public Affairs (Amherst, Mass.), vol. 1, no. 1 (October 1959), pp. 5-24.
Includes Frost's poem "Somewhat Dietary" in facsimile and printed text on p. 24.
Rare Book Room PS3511.R94 Z9193 1959

Slyshu, Poet Amerika: Poetry SSha.
Moskva: Izd-vo Inostrannoi Lit-ry, 1960.
Includes Russian translations of poetry by Robert Frost, pp. 42-44.
Rare Book Room PS619.R8 S59 1960

Sohn, David A. and Tyre, Richard H.
Frost; the Poet and His Poetry.
New York: Holt, Rinehart and Winston, c1967.
"This book and the film, 'A Lover's Quarrel with the World,' are designed for a one-week or possible two-week unit on Robert Frost." Includes selections from Frost's verse and prose.
Rare Book Room PS3511.R94 Z9245 (2 copies)

Sohn, David A. and Tyre, Richard H.
Frost; the Poet and His Poetry.
New York: Bantam, c1969.
Special revised edition. "Annotated bibliography": pp. 128-131.
Rare Book Room PS3511.R94 Z9245 1969

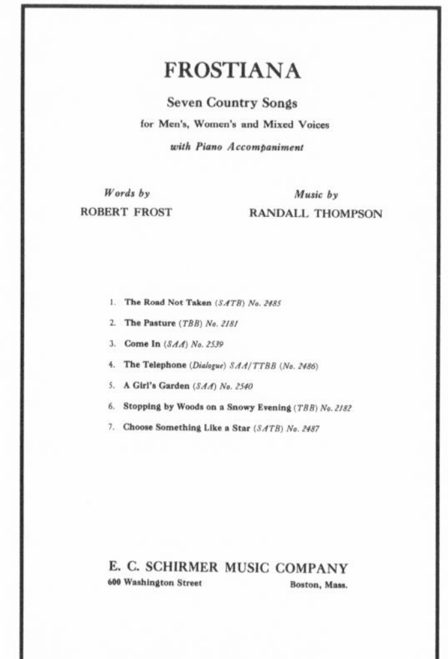
FROSTIANA
Seven Country Songs
for Men's, Women's and Mixed Voices
with Piano Accompaniment

Words by ROBERT FROST
Music by RANDALL THOMPSON

1. The Road Not Taken (*SATB*) *No. 2485*
2. The Pasture (*TBB*) *No. 2181*
3. Come In (*SAA*) *No. 2539*
4. The Telephone (*Dialogue*) *SAA/TTBB* (*No. 2486*)
5. A Girl's Garden (*SAA*) *No. 2540*
6. Stopping by Woods on a Snowy Evening (*TBB*) *No. 2182*
7. Choose Something Like a Star (*SATB*) *No. 2487*

E. C. SCHIRMER MUSIC COMPANY
600 Washington Street Boston, Mass.

Seven Country Songs. (Frostiana) New York:E.C Shirmer Music Co., 1959-60. Commissioned in 1958 for the 200th anniversary of Amherst, Massachusetts.

Stegner, Wallace.
Robert Frost & Bernard DeVoto.
[s.l.]: The Associates of the Stanford University Libraries, 1974.
Limited to "125 copies printed for the Roxburghe Club of San Francisco." Includes facsimilie of letter to "Benny" from Robert Frost. "Published on the occasion of the Robert Frost Centennial Exhibit, April 28-August 31, 1974, by The Associates of the Stanford University Libraries."
Rare Book Room PS3511.R94 Z927 1974 (2 copies)

These Things the Poets Said.
Flansham, England: The Pear Tree Press, 1935.
Limited to 145 numbered copies. Library's copy is number 145. Includes a tribute, "To E. T." [Edward Thomas] by Robert Frost on p. 16.
Rare Book Room PR6039.H55 Z83 1935

Thomas, Edward.
The Flowers I Love: A Series of Twenty-four Drawings in Colour by Katharine Cameron with an Anthology of Flower Poems Selected by Edward Thomas.
London: T. C. & E. C. Jack, n.d.

Includes 3 poems by Robert Frost on pages (6-7), (42-43), and (71-72). Anthology of poems selected by Edward Thomas to go with 24 drawings of Cameron.

THE PASTURE*

I'm going out to clean the pasture spring;
I'll only stop to rake the leaves away
(And wait to watch the water clear, I may):
I sha'n't be gone long. — You come too.

I'm going out to fetch the little calf
That's standing by the mother. It's so young
It totters when she licks it with her tongue.
I sha'n't be gone long. — You come too.

ROBERT FROST

Thompson, Randall.
Frostiana; Seven Country Songs for Men's, Women's, and Mixed Voices, with Piano Accompaniment.
Music by Randall Thompson; words by Robert Frost.
Boston: E. C. Schirmer, 1959.

Contents: The Road Not Taken; The Pasture; Come In; The Telephone; A Girl's Garden; Stopping by Woods on a Snowy Evening; Choose Something Like a Star. Publisher's numbers 2485, 2181, 2539, 2486, 2540, 2182, 2487 respectively.

Untermeyer, Louis.
"—and Other Poets."
Frontispiece by George Wolfe Plank.
New York: Henry Holt and Company, 1916.
1st edition. Parodies, in verse, reprinted in part from various periodicals. Includes the poem "Death of the Tired Man" by Robert Frost (pp. 22-25).
Rare Book Room PS3541.N72 A8 1916

Untermeyer, Louis.
Heavens.
New York: Harcourt, Brace and Company, c1922.
Includes the poem "The Sagging Bough" by Robert Frost on p. 128. Library's copy is signed by the author.
Rare Book Room PS3541.N72 H4 1922

Untermeyer, Louis.
Including Horace.
New York: Harcourt, Brace and Howe, 1919.
"The present volume is an effort to do two things: first to suggest, through the thin veil of parody, how certain other poets would have used Horatian subjects—and one famous theme in particular. Second, to present, in a loose set of paraphrases, the spirit rather than the letter of most of Horace's finest odes." Includes the poem "Takes it up to New Hampshire" by Robert Frost (pp. 30-31) Dust jacket.
Rare Book Room PS3541.N72 I6 1919

Untermeyer, Louis.
Play in Poetry: The Henry Ward Beecher Lectures Delivered at Amherst College October, 1987.
New York: Harcourt, Brace and Company, c1938.
First edition. "The first four chapters of this volume were delivered as lectures in Johnson Chapel at Amherst College during October, 1937, on the Henry Ward Beecher Foundation." (p. v.) Dedicated to Robert Frost. Includes selections from "Collected Poems" and "A Further Range" by Robert Frost. Review copy, 3/3/38.
Rare Book Room PN1064 .U5 1938

Untermeyer, Louis.
Robert Frost: A Backward Look.
Washington, D.C.: Library of Congress, 1964.

Untermeyer, Louis.
Robert Frost: A Backward Look.
Washington: Reference Dept., Library of Congress; [for sale by the Superintendent of Documents, U.S. Govt. Print. Off.], 1964.

Includes excerpts from Frost's poetry. "A lecture presented under the auspices of the Gertrude Clarke Whittall Poetry and Literature Fund, with selective bibliography of Frost Manuscripts, separately published works, recordings, and motion pictures in the collections of the Library of Congress."

Rare Book Room PS3511.R94 Z965 1964 (5 copies)

Washington, D.C. Inaugural Committee, 1961.
Official Program, Inaugural Ceremonies of John F. Kennedy, Thirty-fifth President of the United States and Lyndon B. Johnson, Thirty-seventh Vice President of the United States. Washington, D. C., January 20, 1961.
[Washington: s.n], c1961.

Contains contributions by Robert Frost: "A New England Tribute" on p. 43 of the Official Inaugural Program and a "Dedicatory Poem" written especially for the Inauguration on p. 14 of the Pictorial Review. Library's copy is number 349 of the Limited Deluxe Edition. Leatherette cover stamped Frank P. Piskor.

Rare Book Room F200 .W3

[52] *What Cheer: An Anthology of American and British Humorous and Witty Verse, Gathered, Sifted, and Salted.*
Introduction by David McCord.
New York: Coward-McCann Inc., c1945.
First edition. Includes poems by Robert Frost: "Brown's Descent," "A Considerable Speck," "A Correction," and "The Hardship of Accounting." Dust jacket. Library's copy has three line inscription by Frost to Earl Burnheimer.
Rare Book Room PR1195.H8 W5 1945

Whicher, George F.
Mornings at 8:50: Brief Evocations of the Past for a College Audience.
Northampton, MA: Published by the Hampshire Bookshop for the Trustees of Amherst College, 1950.
Includes the poem "Goodbye and Keep Cold" by Robert Frost on pp. 37-38. Dust jacket.
Rare Book Room LD152.9 .W48 1950

Widdemer, Margaret.
A Tree With a Bird In It: A Symposium of Contemporary American Poets on Being Shown a Pear-Tree on Which Sat a Grackle.
New York: Harcourt, Brace and Company, c1922.
Includes the poem "The Bird Misunderstood" by Robert Frost on page 12. Library's copy inscribed: "To Frank Piskor 1963" by author.
Rare Book Room PS3545.I175 T7 1922

Wilkinson, Marguerite.
New Voices: An Introduction to Contemporary Poetry.
New York: The Macmillan Company, 1923, [c1921]
New edition revised and enlarged. Includes several poems by Robert Frost.
Rare Book Room PR601.W5 1921

Wilkinson, Marguerite.
The Way of the Makers.
New York: The Macmillan Company, 1925.
Includes a commentary by Robert Frost (p. 207).
Rare Book Room PN1042 .W5 1925

WORKS ABOUT OR INCLUDING WORKS ABOUT FROST

Allegheny College Library.
An Exhibition of the Work of Robert Frost: In Connection With the Opening of The John Scott Craig Reading Room in the Reis Library and the Delivery of The John C. Sturtevant Lecture.
Meadville, PA: Allegheny College, 1938.
Rare Book Room PS3511.R94 Z459 1938

Anderson, George Kumler.
Bread Loaf School of English: the First Fifty Years.
[Middlebury, VT]: Middlebury College Press, 1969.
Rare Book Room LD3311.M32 A73 1969

Anderson, Margaret Bartlett.
Robert Frost and John Bartlett: The Record of a Friendship.
New York: Holt, Rinehart and Winston, c1963.
First edition. Copy 3 has inscription to Frank Piskor from the author. Copies 2 and 3 in dust jacket.
Rare Book Room PS3511.R94 Z57 (2 copies)

Ando, Ichiro.
Robert Frost.
[Tokyo: Kenkyusha Publishing Co.], 1958.
Bound in yellow cloth; stamped in black. Dust jacket.
Rare Book Room PS3511.R94 Z5488 1958 (2 copies)

August, June and Peterson, Arthur.
Robert Frost - Fire and Ice.
Auburn, CA: Audio Partners, c1990.
An unabridged recording of the play. Presents Arthur Peterson as Robert Frost in a one-man show about the poet's life and career. Includes readings of thirteen of Mr. Frost's poems and a scene from his play entitled "A Masque of Reason."
Rare Book Room PS3511.R94 Z5489 1990

Bishop, John Peale.
Antologia de Escritores Contemporaneos de los Estados Unidos [Anthology of Contemporary Writers of the United States].
Santiago, Chile: Editorial Nascimento, 1944.
Spanish edition. Prosa y verso compilados por John Peale Bishop y Allen Tate; version de la prosa a cargo de Ricardo A. Latcham; version de la poesia a cargo de varios traductores. Contains, for the most part, selections included in the *American Harvest*, edited by Allen Tate and John Peale Bishop. Includes 2 poems by Frost on pp [422]-429 of vol. 1. The sections of poetry have Spanish and English on opposite pages.
Rare Book Room PS525.S7 B5 (2 vols.)

Blumenthal, Joseph.
Robert Frost and the Spiral Press.
[New York: Spiral Press, 1963]
Four hundred and fifty copies printed. Issued as holiday greetings, Dec. 1964, by Ann and Joseph Blumenthal.
Rare Book Room PS3511.R94 Z554 1963 (2 copies)

Bober, Natalie S.
A Restless Spirit: The Story of Robert Frost.
New York: Henry Holt and Company, c1991.
Revised and expanded edition. "A biography of the famous American poet, detailing the events of his frequently unhappy life, his love for his wife and children, and the way all of this was woven into his poetry." Dust jacket.
Rare Book Room PS3511.R94 Z555 1991

Borroff, Marie.
Language and the Poet: Verbal Artistry in Frost, Stevens, and Moore.
Chicago: University of Chicago Press, c1979.
Dust jacket.
Rare Book Room PS323.5 .B64 1979

Bread Loaf Book of Plays.
Edited by Hortense Moore; introduction by John Mason Brown.
Middlebury, VT: Middlebury College Press, 1941.
Includes the play "Snow" which is a dramatization of Robert Frost's poem on pp. 1-18.
Rare Book Room PN6120.A4 B73 1941

Breit, Harvey.
The Writer Observed.
Cleveland and New York: World Publishing Company, c1956.
Second printing. Includes selection about Robert Frost on pp. 95-97. Dust jacket.
Rare Book Room PR473 .B72 c.2

Brewer, Wilmon.
Talks About Poetry.
Francestown, NH: Marshall Jones Company, c1948.
Dust jacket.
Rare Book Room PN1470 .B7 1948

Brooks, Van Wyck.
New England: Indian Summer, 1865-1915.
[New York]: E. P. Dutton & Co., Inc., 1940.
First edition. Includes several references to Robert Frost.
Rare Book Room PS243 .B72 1940 c.2

Brooks, Van Wyck.
On Literature Today.
New York: E. P. Dutton & Co., Inc., 1941.
First edition. "This address was delivered at the inauguration of Dr. George N. Shuster as president of Hunter College, New York, October 10th, 1940." Includes comments on Robert Frost's works on pp. 12-13. Dust jacket.
Rare Book Room PS221 .B75 1941

Brower, Reuben Arthur.
The Poetry of Robert Frost: Constellations of Intention.
New York: Oxford University Press, 1963.
Dust jacket.
Rare Book Room PS3511.R94 Z556 1963

Burnshaw, Stanley.
Robert Frost Himself.
New York: George Braziller, c1986.
Copies 2 and 3 in dust jacket.
Rare Book Room PS3511.R94 Z558 1986 (2 copies)

 Byers, Edna Hanley.
Robert Frost at Agnes Scott College.
Decatur, GA: McCain Library, Agnes Scott College, 1963.
A bibliography of Frost holdings at Agnes Scott College. Includes discography (pp. 66-68).
Rare Book Room PS3511.R94 Z459 1963

Cane, Melville.
"Robert Frost, an Intermittent Intimacy," in *The American Scholar* (Chicago, IL), Winter 1970-71, pp. 158-166.
Rare Book Room PS3511.R94 Z559

A Casebook on Ezra Pound.
Edited by William Van O'Connor and Edward Stone.
New York: Thomas Y. Crowell Company, c1959.
Rare Book Room PS3531.O82 Z78 c.4

Ciardi, John.
Dialogue With An Audience.
Philadelphia and New York: J. B. Lippincott Company, c1963.
First edition. Includes 3 articles about Robert Frost on pp. [149]-195. Copies 1 and 2 in dust jacket.
Rare Book Room PN1064 .C5 1963 (2 copies)

Clark, Keith.
The Muse Colony:
Rupert Brooke, Edward Thomas, Robert Frost, and Friends.
Bristol [Eng.]: Redcliffe, 1992.
Includes a chapter on Robert Frost with several of his poems (pp. 61-75).
Rare Book Room PR601.C527 1992

Clemens, Cyril.
A Chat with Robert Frost.
Foreword by Hamlin Garland.
[Folcroft, PA]: Folcroft Library Editions, 1972.
Limited to 150 copies. Reprint of the 1940 edition published by the International Mark Twain Society, Webster Groves, Mo., which was issued as no. 9 of its Biographical series.
Rare Book Room PS3511.R94 Z56 1972

Robert Frost

ROBERT FROST

A Bibliography

BY W. B. SHUBRICK CLYMER AND CHARLES

R. GREEN · FOREWORD BY DAVID LAMBUTH

PUBLISHED IN 1937 AT AMHERST · MASSA-

CHUSETTS BY THE JONES LIBRARY · INC

Clymer, W.B. Shubrick and Green, Charles R. *Robert Frost: A Bibliography*. Amherst: Jones Library, 1937. Copy 3 of 150 signed by Frost. Review copy dated 3/19/37.

Clifton Waller Barrett Library.
Robert Frost: A Descriptive Catalogue of Books and Manuscripts in the Clifton Waller Barrett Library, University of Virginia.
Compiled by Joan St. C. Crane.
Charlottesville, VA: Published for the Associates of the University of Virginia Library by the University Press of Virginia, c1974.
Rare Book Room PS3511.R94 Z565 1974

Clymer, William Branford Shubrick and Green, Charles R.
Robert Frost: A Bibliography.
Foreword by David Lambuth.
Amherst, MA: Jones Library, Inc., 1937.

> "This bibliography of the work of Robert Frost has been issued in a limited edition of six hundred and fifty copies of which the first one hundred and fifty were printed on hand-made paper, especially bound and numbered, and signed by Mr. Frost." Copy 2 is number 149. Copy 3 is "Advance copy for review" dated 3/19/37.

Rare Book Room PS3511.R94 Z575 (2 copies)

 Coffin, Robert P. Tristram.
New Poetry of New England: Frost and Robinson.
Baltimore: The Johns Hopkins Press, 1938.
Lectures delivered in the Percy Turnbull Memorial Lecturship at the Johns Hopkins University.
Rare Book Room PS3511.R94 Z58 1938

Cook, Reginald Lansing.
The Dimensions of Robert Frost.
New York: Rinehart & Company, Inc., c1958.
Inscribed to Frank Piskor by author. Dust jacket.
Rare Book Room PS3511.R94 Z585

Cornell, Julien D.
The Trial of Ezra Pound: A Documented Account of the Treason Case.
New York: John Day Company, c1966.
"Appendix IV. Transcript of trial; transcript of hearing in the United States District Court for the District of Columbia, February 13, 1946," pp. 154-215. Dust jacket.
Rare Book Room PS3531.O82 Z65x c.2

Cox, Sidney.
Robert Frost: Original "Ordinary Man."
New York: Henry Holt and Company, c1929.
1000 copies printed and signed by the author. Binding: dark brown paper covered boards. Backed with white paper covered boards. Dust jacket.
Rare Book Room PS3511.R94 Z59 1929

Dartmouth College Library.
Fifty Years of Robert Frost:
A Catalogue of the Exhibition Held in Baker Library in the Autumn of 1943.
Edited by Ray Nash.
Hanover, NH: Dartmouth College Library, 1944.
Copy 2 is inscribed to Frank Piskor by Ray Nash.
Rare Book Room PS3511.R94 Z459 1944 (2 copies)

Dartmouth College Library.
Under that Arch: A Keepsake Issued by the Dartmouth College Library on the Occasion of the Opening of its Robert Frost Room, April 19, 1962.
[n.p.], 1962.
Rare Book Room PS3511.R94 Z63 1962 (3 copies)

D'Avanzo, Mario L.
A Cloud of Other Poets: Robert Frost and the Romantics.
Lanham, MD: University Press of America, c1991.
Rare Book Room PS3511.R94 Z614 1991

Di Cesare, Mario A.
Poetry and Prophecy: Reflections on the Word.
Amherst, MA: Published for the Friends of the Amherst College Library, c1977.
The Robert Frost lecture, April 9, 1976.
Rare Book Room BS1198 .D53 (2 copies)

Dierkes, Henry.
Robert Frost: A Friend to a Younger Poet.
Introduction by Milton Hindus.
Notasulga, AL: Armstrong Press, 1984.
"An edition of three hundred copies has been printed."
Rare Book Room PS3511.R94 Z617 1984

Doyle, John Robert.
The Poetry of Robert Frost, an Analysis.
Johannesburg: Witwatersrand University Press; New York: Hafner Publishing Co., 1962.
Dust jacket.
Rare Book Room PS3511.R94 Z62 1962 c.2

Elizabethan Studies and Other Essays: In Honor of George F. Reynolds.
Boulder, CO: University of Colorado Studies, 1945.
Includes chapter on Robert Frost, pp. 370-381. University of Colorado Studies, Series B, Studies in the Humanities: vol. 2, no. 4.
Rare Book Room PR651.E55 1945

 Engle, Paul.
Robert Frost.
[Iowa City: State University of Iowa Library, 1959]
Limited to 3000 copies "distributed by The State University of Iowa Library on the occasion of Mr. Frost's visit to the University, April 13, 1959, during National Library Week."
Rare Book Room PS3509.N44 R6 1959 (2 copies)

Faber, Doris.
Robert Frost, America's Poet.
Illustrated by Paul Frame.
Englewood Cliffs, NJ: Prentice-Hall, Inc., c1964.
P-H junior research books. Dust jacket.
Rare Book Room PS3511.R94 Z64

Fisher, Dorothy Canfield.
Vermont Tradition: The Biography of an Outlook on Life.
Boston: Little, Brown and Company, c1953.
Includes commentary about Robert Frost on pp. 383-392. Dust jacket.
Rare Book Room F49 .F57

Ford, Caroline.
The Less Traveled Road: A Study of Robert Frost.
Cambridge, MA: Harvard University Press, 1935.
Radcliffe Honors Theses in English: No. 4.
Rare Book Room PS3511.R94 Z65 1935

Francis, Robert, Cole, Charles W. and Cook, Reginald L.
"On Robert Frost," in *The Massachusetts Review* (Amherst, MA), 4:2, Winter 1963, pp. 237-249.
Rare Book Room PS3511.R94 Z8562

Francis, Robert.
Pot Shots at Poetry.
Ann Arbor: University of Michigan Press, c1980.
Includes a selection on Robert Frost "Frost as Mugwump," pp. 30-31.
Rare Book Room PS3511.R237 P6 1980

Francis, Robert.
Robert Frost: A Time to Talk,
Conversations and Indiscretions Recorded by Robert Francis.
[London]: Robson Books, c1972.
Dust jacket.
Rare Book Room PS3511.R94 Z653 1973

Fraser, Marjorie Frost.
Franconia.
[New York]: Spiral Press, 1936.
Inscribed to Frank Piskor by Lesley Frost Ballantine, January 17, 1977.
Rare Book Room PS3511.R335 F7 1936

Frederic G. Melcher:
Friendly Reminiscences of a Half Century Among Books & Bookmen.
New York: The Book Publishers' Bureau, 1945.
Library's copy has inscription to Frank Piskor by author. Dust jacket.
Rare Book Room Z473.M45 F74 1945

Frost: Centennial Essays.
Jackson: University Press of Mississippi, 1974.
Second printing (with minor corrections) compiled by the Committee on the Frost Centennial of the University of Southern Mississippi. Library's copy has inscription to Frank Piskor by Lesley Frost.
Rare Book Room PS3511.R94 Z654 1974

Frost: Centennial Essays II.
Edited by Jac Tharpe.
Jackson: University Press of Mississippi, 1976.
Copies 1 and 2 have inscription to Frank Piskor by Lesley Frost.
Rare Book Room PS3511.R94 Z6544 (2 copies)

Frost: Centennial Essays III.
Edited by Jac Tharpe.
Jackson: University Press of Mississippi, 1978.
Library's copy has inscription to Frank Piskor by Lesley Frost. Dust jacket.
Rare Book Room PS3511.R94 Z6545

Frost, Lesley.
Going on Two: Poems.
Drawings by Robin Hudnut.
Old Greenwich, CT: The Devin-Adair Company, c1973.
Copy 2 is inscribed to Frank Piskor by the author.
Rare Book Room PS3511.R924 G6 (2 copies)

Frost, Lesley.
Really Not Really.
Illustrated by Barbara Remington.
Manhasset, NY: Channel Press, Inc., c1962.
Dust jacket.
Rare Book Room PS3511.R924 R42 1962

Gethyn-Jones, J. E.
Dymock Down the Ages.
Foreword by Earl Beauchamp.
Dymock (Glos.): Rev. J. E. Gethyn-Jones, [1966]
[Revised ed.] Map on endpapers. Dust jacket.
Rare Book Room DA690.D98 G4 1966

Gethyn-Jones, J. E.
Robert Frost - 6th June 1957.
Syracuse: Syracuse University Library Associates, 1969.
First separate and limited edition.
Rare Book Room PS3511.R94 Z667 1969 (6 copies)

Gibson, Wilfred.
Hazards.
London: Macmillan, 1930.
Dedicated to Robert and Elinor Frost. Dust jacket.
Rare Book Room PR6013.I29 H3 1930

Glaenzer, Richard Butler.
Literary Snapshots, Impressions of Contemporary Authors.
New York: Brentano's, c1920.
Reprinted in part from the *Atlantic Monthly* and *The Bookman.* Includes literary "snapshot" about Robert Frost on p. 100.
Rare Book Room PS3513.L2 L5 1920

Gone Into If Not Explained: Essays On Poems by Robert Frost.
Edited by Greg Kuzma.
Crete, NE: Best Cellar Press, c1976.
A special double issue of *Pebble*, Nos. 14 & 15.
Rare Book Room PS3511.R94 G66 1976 (2 copies)

Gould, Jean.
Robert Frost; the Aim Was Song.
New York: Dodd, Mead & Company, c1964.
Copy 2 has inscription to Frank Piskor by the author. Dust jacket.
Rare Book Room PS3511.R94 Z68 c.2

Grade, Arnold E.
The Outset, and Other Poems.
Foreword by Herbert Slusser.
St. Paul, MN: College of St. Thomas, c1959.
Includes poem "On a Visit With a Poet" about Robert Frost.
Rare Book Room PS3513.R4135 O9 1959

Grade, Arnold E.
A Robert Frost Folio.
[United States: s.n., between 1949 and 1969]
Issued in an envelope.
Rare Book Room PS3511.R94 Z683

Grant, Douglas.
Robert Frost and His Reputation.
London and New York: Cambridge University Press, [1965].
Australian Humanities Research Council. Occasional paper no. 7.
Rare Book Room PS3511.R94 Z685 1965

Graves, Robert, 1895-
Oxford Addresses on Poetry.
Garden City, NY: Doubleday & Company, 1962.
First edition in U.S.A. Includes chapter containing correspondence with Robert Frost.
Rare Book Room PR503 .G68 1962

Greiner, Donald J.
The Merrill Guide to Robert Frost.
Columbus, OH: Charles E. Merrill Publishing Company, c1969.
Rare Book Room PS3511.R94 Z72 1969

Greiner, Donald J.
Robert Frost: The Poet and His Critics.
Chicago: American Library Association, 1974.
Rare Book Room PS3511.R94 Z73 c.2

Grove, Victor.
The Language Bar.
[London]: Routeledge & Kegan Paul, [1950]
Rare Book Room PE1075 .G75 1950

Hall, Donald.
An Evening's Frost.
New York: Judith Marechal Productions, [1964]

"An Evening's Frost was the first dramatic treatment of the poet to be authorized by the literary executor of the Frost estate after his death. Commissioned in 1964 by the University of Michigan Professional Theatre Program..." Includes performance program.

Rare Book Room PS3515.A3152 E9

Hall, Donald.
Remembering Poets: Reminiscences and Reflections: Dylan Thomas, Robert Frost, T. S. Eliot, Ezra Pound.
New York: Harper & Row, c1978.
First edition. Copy 2 has inscription to Frank Piskor by the author.
Rare Book Room PS3515.A3152 Z526 c.2

Hall, Donald.
Their Ancient Glittering Eyes: Remembering Poets and More Poets: Robert Frost, Dylan Thomas, T.S. Eliot, Archibald MacLeish, Yvor Winters, Marianne Moore, Ezra Pound.
New York: Ticknor & Fields, 1992.

Revised and enlarged edition of *Remembering Poets*, c1978. Includes chapter entitled "Vanity, Fame, Love, and Robert Frost," pp. 13-44. Library's copy has inscription by author. Dust jacket.

Rare Book Room PS3515.A3152 Z526 1992

Hall, Dorothy Judd.
Robert Frost: Contours of Belief.
Athens, OH: Ohio University Press, c1984.
Rare Book Room PS3511.R94 Z74 1984 c.2

Hard, Margaret.
A Memory of Vermont; Our Life in the Johnny Appleseed Bookshop, 1930-1965.
New York: Harcourt, Brace & World, Inc., c1967.
First edition. Includes anecdotes "about a great diversity of people, among them" Robert Frost. Dust jacket.
Rare Book Room Z473.J68 H3 c.2

Hillyer, Robert.
A Letter to Robert Frost and Others.
New York: Alfred A. Knopf, 1937.
First edition. Copies 2 and 3 in dust jacket.
Rare Book Room PS3515.I69 L4 1937 (3 copies)

Holmes, John.
The Symbols.
Wood engravings by John De Pol.
Iowa City: The Prairie Press, c1955.
Includes the poem "Anecdote of Robert Frost" on p. 13.
Rare Book Room PS3511.O4445 S9 1955

In Fealty to Apollo: Poetry Society of America, 1910-1950.
Edited & compiled by Gustav Davidson, with a chronicle by A. M. Sullivan and foreword by Robert Hillyer.
New York: Fine Editions Press, 1950.
Dust jacket.
Rare Book Room PS301.P67 I5 1950

An Institute of Modern Literature at Bowdoin College, Brunswick, Maine, from May 5 to May 16, 1925, in Commemoration of the Centennial Year of the Graduation of the Class of 1825.
Lewiston, ME: Lewiston Journal Company, 1926.
Comments, by A. G. Staples, in *Lewiston Evening Journal*, concerning the contributions of Robert Frost, Edna St. Vincent Millay, Carl Sandburg, James Stephens, Willa Cather, John Dos Passos, and others.
Rare Book Room LD557.7 1926

 International Literary Annual, No. 1.
Edited by John Wain.
London: John Calder, c1958.
Dust jacket.
Rare Book Room PN12.I5

International Literary Annual, No. 2.
Edited by John Wain.
New York: Criterion Books, c1959.
Includes in the 'Literary Awards' section on p. 230 an entry noting that Robert Frost received the Alexander Droutzkoy Memorial Award from the Poetry Society. Dust jacket.
Rare Book Room PS3511.R94 Z748

Iowa University. Poetry Workshop.
West of Boston; Poems from the State University of Iowa Poetry Workshop in Honor of the Visit of Robert Frost.
Iowa City: Qara Press, [1959]
Edition limited to 400 copies. Bound in white paper wrappers, title printed on front cover.
Rare Book Room PS571.I8 I52 1959 (2 copies)

Isaacs, Elizabeth.
An Introduction to Robert Frost.
Denver: Alan Swallow, c1962.
Dust jacket.
Rare Book Room PS3511.R94 Z75 1962

Jamieson, Paul F.
"Robert Frost, Poet of Mountain Land" in *Appalachia* (Boston, MA) 25:12, Dec. 15, 1959, pp. 471-479.
Rare Book Room PS3511.R94 Z753

Jarrell, Randall.
Poetry and the Age.
London: Faber and Faber Limited, [1955]
Dust jacket.
Rare Book Room PN1271 .J3 1955

Jennings, Elizabeth.
Frost.
Edinburgh: Oliver and Boyd, c1964, 1966.
Rare Book Room PS3511.R94 Z755 1964 (3 copies)

Kahn, Roger.
How the Weather Was.
New York: Harper & Row, c1973.
First edition. A selection of the author's profiles and articles from the world of sports, music, and literature. Includes selection about Robert Frost on pp. [109]-126. Dust jacket.
Rare Book Room CT220 .K33 c.2

Katz, Sandra L.
Elinor Frost, a Poet's Wife.
Westfield, MA: Institute for Massachusetts Studies, Westfield State College, 1988.
Dust jacket.
Rare Book Room PS3511.R94 Z7575 1988 c.2

Kemp, John C.
Robert Frost and New England: The Poet as Regionalist.
Princeton, NJ: Princeton University Press, c1979.
Based on the author's doctoral dissertation, University of Pennsylvania. Dust jacket.
Rare Book Room PS3511.R94 Z758 1979

Katz, Sandra. *Elinor Frost: A Poet's Wife.* Westfield, MA: Institute for Massachusetts Studies, Westfield State College, 1988. Elinor Frost White graduated from St. Lawrence University in 1895.

ROBERT
FROST 100

During the centennial year of the poet's birth one hundred items representative of his books and other printed works have been chosen to form a traveling exhibit projected in tribute to Robert Frost's achievements as an author and in commemoration also of certain of his friendships and associations over the years.

Compiled by Edward Connery Lathem

DAVID R. GODINE · PUBLISHER
BOSTON · MASSACHUSETTS · 1974

Latham, Edward, compiler
Robert Frost 100.
Boston: David Godine, 1974.
Inscribed "For Frank Piskor / Archibald MacLeish / November 1974."

Lathem, Edward Connery and Lawrance Thompson.
Robert Frost and the Lawrence, Massachusetts, High School Bulletin: the Beginning of a Literary Career.
New York: Grolier Club, 1966.

Limited to 1200 copies. "The facsimile section reproduces in full each of the four issues of the Lawrence High School bulletin for the period of Robert Frost's editorship."

Rare Book Room PS3511.R94 Z7642 c.2

Lathem, Edward Connery.
Robert Frost 100.
Boston, MA: David R. Godine, 1974.

Catalogue of 100 items representative of Frost's printed works which formed a traveling exhibit, May-December 1974 at Princeton University Library and others, commemorating the centennial of Frost's birth. Copy 1 in dust jacket.

Rare Book Room PS3511.R94 Z7643 1974 (2 copies)

Library of Congress. General Reference and Bibliography Division.
Literary Recordings; a Checklist of the Archive of Recorded Poetry and Literature in the Library of Congress.
Washington: [For sale by the Supt. of Docs., U.S. Govt. Print. Off.], 1966.

"Brings up through June 1965 the inventory of the Library's spoken recordings that were first listed in its Archive of recorded poetry and literature: a checklist." Includes entries for the recorded poetry of Robert Frost held by the archive.

Rare Book Room PS306.5.Z9 U53 1966 c.2

Lentricchia, Frank.
Robert Frost: Modern Poetics and the Landscapes of Self.
Durham, NC: Duke University Press, 1975.

Dust jacket.

Rare Book Room PS3511.R94 Z7644 1975

Levine, David.
Literary Caricatures: From the New York Review of Books.
New York: The New York Review, Inc., c1964.

Includes caricature of Robert Frost on p. 1.

Rare Book Room NC1429.L47 A5 (3 copies)

Lowell, Amy.
A Critical Fable.
Boston: Houghton Mifflin, 1922.

"by a poker of fun."

Rare Book Room PS3523.088 C75 1922 (2 copies)

Lynen, John F.
The Pastoral Art of Robert Frost.
New Haven: Yale University Press, 1960.

Yale studies in English; 147. Dust jacket.

Rare Book Room PS3511.R94 Z77 1960 c.2

McCurdy, Michael.
Toward the Light: Wood Engravings.
Erin, Ont.: Porcupine's Quill; Scarborough, Ont.: Distributed by Firefly Books, c1982.

Contains woodcut of Robert Frost (number 32)

Rare Book Room NE539.M22 T6 1982

MacLeish, Archibald.
A Continuing Journey.
Boston: Houghton Mifflin, 1968. [c1967]
Copy 2 has inscription to Frank Piskor by the author. Includes selection about Robert Frost on pp. [299]-306. Dust jacket.
Rare Book Room PS3525.A27 C69 c.2

McLeish, Archibald.
Letters of Archibald MacLeish, 1907 to 1982.
Edited by R. H. Winnick.
Boston, MA: Houghton Mifflin, 1983.
Includes letters to Robert Frost. Dust jacket.
Rare Book Room PS3525.A27 Z48 1983

MacNeice, Louis.
Varieties of Parable.
Cambridge [Eng.]: University Press, 1965.
Clark lectures, Trinity College, Cambridge University, 1963. Dust jacket.
Rare Book Room PN56.A5 M3 1965

Madison, Charles A.
Irving to Irving: Author-Publisher Relations, 1800-1974.
New York: R. R. Bowker Company, 1974.
Includes chapter on Robert Frost's relations with Holt Co. on pp. 65-80. Dust jacket.
Rare Book Room PN155 .M27 1974

Madison, Charles A.
The Owl Among Colophons: Henry Holt as Publisher and Editor.
New York: Holt, Rinehart and Winston, c1966.
First edition. Includes a chapter on Holt relations with Robert Frost on pp. 165-185. Dust jacket.
Rare Book Room Z473.H75 M3 1966 (2 copies)

The Major American Poets: An Introduction.
[S.l.: s.n.], 1989.
Rare Book Room PS586 .M35 1989

Marcus, Mordecai.
The Poems of Robert Frost: An Explication.
Boston, MA: G. K. Hall, c1991.
Rare Book Room PS3511.R94 Z785 1991 c.2

Mayhead, Robin.
Understanding Literature.
Cambridge [Eng.]: University Press, 1965.
Dust jacket.
Rare Book Room PR83 .M39 c.2

Melcher, Frederic Gershom.
"Robert Frost and His Books," in *The Colophon: A Book Collectors' Quarterly* (New York), Part two, May 1930.
Also includes: "A bibliography of Robert Frost compiled by H.S. Boutell" which follows Melcher's article.
Rare Book Room PS3511.R94 Z7858

Mertins, Louis, and Mertins, Esther.
The Intervals of Robert Frost: A Critical Bibliography.
Introduction by Fulmer Mood.
Berkeley: University of California Press, 1947.
Rare Book Room PS3511.R94 Z786 1947

Mertins, Louis.
Robert Frost; Life and Talks-Walking.
Norman, OK: University of Oklahoma Press, c1965.
First edition. Dust jacket.
Rare Book Room PS3511.R94 Z786 1965

Middlebury College.
Robert Frost.
Middlebury, VT: Middlebury College, c1954.
A booklet of photographs honoring Frost "on the occasion of his eightieth birthday." Copy 1 is number 713, copy 2 is number 895, copy 3 is number 896, copy 4 is number 821, copy 5 is number 717, and copy 6 is number 820. Copy 4 contains, on the inside front cover, 4 First day of issue "Robert Frost, American Poet" stamps (10 cents), postmarked Derry, NH, March 26, 1974.
Rare Book Room PS3511.R94 Z789 1954 (6 copies)

 Monteiro, George.
Robert Frost & the New England Renaissance.
[Lexington, KY]: University Press of Kentucky, c1988.
Dust jacket.
Rare Book Room PS3511.R94 Z793 1988 c.2

Moody, William Vaughn and Lovett, Robert Morss.
A History of English Literature, from Beowulf to 1926.
New York: Charles Scribner's Sons, c1926.
[Rev. ed.] "Reading guide": pp. 491-522.
Rare Book Room PR85 .M615 1926

Moody, William Vaughn.
Letters to Harriet.
Edited with introduction and conclusion by Percy MacKaye.
Boston: Houghton Mifflin, 1935.
The letters cover the years of Moody's life from 1901 to his marriage in 1909. Includes commentary on Robert Frost.
Rare Book Room PS2428 .A47 1935 (2 copies)

Morrison, Kathleen.
Robert Frost; a Pictorial Chronicle.
New York: Holt, Rinehart and Winston, c1974.
Dust jacket.
Rare Book Room PS3511.R94 Z795 (2 copies)

Morrison, Theodore and Cox, Edward Hyde.
Addresses Delivered in Ripton, Vermont on August 20, 1964 at the Dedication of an Historical Marker Honoring Robert Frost.
Hanover, NH: Friends of the Dartmouth Library, 1964.
"The addresses...have been slightly revised from their texts as originally delivered."
Rare Book Room PS3511.R94 Z796 1964

Morrison, Theodore.
Bread Loaf Writers' Conference: The First Thirty Years (1926-1955).
[Middlebury, VT]: Middlebury College Press, 1976.
1 of 12 handbound copies. Includes discussions on Robert Frost's associations with the Bread Loaf Writers' Conference.
Rare Book Room PN133.U5 B734 1976

Mountain Passages: An Appalachia Anthology.
Edited by Robert E. Manning.
Boston, MA: Appalachian Mountain Club, c1982.
First edition. Includes article "Robert Frost: Poet of Mountain Land" on pp. 111-115 by St. Lawrence University professor emeritus, Paul F. Jamieson.
Rare Book Room F106 .M87 1982

Munson, Gorham B.
Robert Frost; A Study in Sensibility and Good Sense.
New York: George H. Doran Company, c1927.
The Murray Hill biographies.
Rare Book Room PS3511.R94 Z8 c.2

Munson, Gorham.
Robert Frost; Making Poems for America.
Illustrated by Dan Siculan.
Chicago: Encyclopaedia Britannica Press, c1962.
Dust jacket.
Rare Book Room PS3511.R94 Z82 1962

Newdick, Robert Spangler.
Newdick's Season of Frost: An Interrupted Biography of Robert Frost.
Edited by William A. Sutton.
Albany: State University of New York Press, 1976.
First edition. Dust jacket.
Rare Book Room PS3511.R94 Z84 1976

Nitchie, George W.
Human Values in the Poetry of Robert Frost, a Study of a Poet's Convictions.
Durham, NC: Duke University Press, 1960.
Dust jacket.
Rare Book Room PS3511.R94 Z85 1960

Norman, Charles.
The Case of Ezra Pound.
New York: Bodley Press, 1948.
Contains a statement by William Carlos Williams. Also contains contributions by e. e. cummings, Louis Zukofsky and Conrad Aiken.
Rare Book Room PS3531.O82 Z77 c.2

 Noon, William T.
Poetry and Prayer.
New Brunswick, NJ: Rutgers University Press, c1967.
Includes a chapter on Robert Frost, pp. [193]-223. Dust jacket.
Rare Book Room PR605.R5 N6 c.2

Orton, Vrest.
Vermont Afternoons With Robert Frost.
Rutland, VT: Charles E. Tuttle Company, 1971.
Dust jacket.
Rare Book Room PS3565.R8 V4 1971

Orton, Vrest.
Vermont Afternoons With Robert Frost.
Rutland, VT: Academy Books, c1979.
Rare Book Room PS3565.R8 V4 1979

Oster, Judith.
Toward Robert Frost: The Reader and the Poet.
Athens: University of Georgia Press, 1991.
Both copies in dust jacket.
Rare Book Room PS3511.R94 Z857 1991 (2 copies)

Parsons, Thornton H.
The Humanism of Robert Frost: A Study in Parallels.
[Ann Arbor]: University of Michigan, 1959.
Library's copy has inscription to Frank Piskor by the author. Spine title: Thornton Parsons on Robert Frost.
Rare Book Room PS3511.R94 Z885 1959

Pierpont Morgan Library.
The Spiral Press Through Four Decades, An Exhibition of Books and Ephemera.
New York: The Pierpont Morgan Library, 1966.
One of 400 copies. Includes a commentary by Joseph Blumenthal and exhibit material on Robert Frost. Bound in gray and blue cloth, stamped in gold. Dust jacket.
Rare Book Room Z473 .P48

Pineda, Rafael.
Robert Frost en los Bosques de Nueva Inglaterra.
Valencia: Universidad de Carabobo, [1960]
Ediciones de la Universidad de Carabobo.
Rare Book Room PS3511.R94 Z62 1960 (3 copies)

Poet to Poet: A Treasury of Golden Criticism.
Edited by Houston Peterson and William S. Lynch.
New York: Prentice-Hall, 1945.
Includes the poem "A Letter to Robert Frost" by Robert Hillyer on pp. 333-339. Dust jacket.
Rare Book Room PN1064.P5 1945

The Poetry of Robert Frost: [Introduction]
Edited by Edward Connery Lathem.
Barre, MA: Imprint Society, 1971.
Includes excerpts from Frost's poetry and correspondence from Frost. Reprint of the "Introduction" section from *The Poetry of Robert Frost*, Vol. 1.
Rare Book Room PS3511 .R94 1971, Intro

Poirier, Richard.
Robert Frost: The Work of Knowing.
New foreword by John Hollander.
Stanford, CA: Stanford University Press, 1990.
Rare Book Room PS3511.R94 Z87 1990

Pritchard, William H.
Frost: A Literary Life Reconsidered.
New York: Oxford University Press, 1984.
Copy 2 has inscription to Frank Piskor by the author. Copy 3 in dust jacket.
Rare Book Room PS3511.R94 Z89 1984 (2 copies)

Rand, Frank Prentice.
The Village of Amherst, a Landmark of Light.
Amherst, MA: Amherst Historical Society, 1958.
Includes commentary on Robert Frost and a picture of his eightieth birthday. Dust jacket.
Rare Book Room F74.A5 R3

Recognition of Robert Frost; Twenty-Fifth Anniversary.
Edited by Richard Thornton.
New York: Henry Holt and Company, c1937.
A collection of many of the important studies and critical analyses that have been made of Mr. Frost and his poetry since 1913, in celebration of the twenty-fifth anniversary of the publication of his first volume. Dust jacket.
Rare Book Room PS3511.R94 Z9 c.2

Reeve, F. D.
Robert Frost in Russia.
Boston: Little, Brown and Company, c1964.
First edition. Dust jacket.
Rare Book Room PS3511.R94 Z914

Robert Frost: A Collection of Critical Essays.
Edited by James M. Cox.
Englewood Cliffs, NJ: Prentice-Hall, Inc., 1962.
Twentieth century views. Dust jacket.
Rare Book Room PS3511.R94 Z588 c.2

Robert Frost, an Introduction.
Edited by Robert A. Greenberg and James G. Hepburn.
New York: Holt, Rinehart and Winston, c1961.
Rare Book Room PS3511.R94 Z7 1961

"Robert Frost: Critical Views and Reminiscences," in *The Southern Review* (Baton Rouge, LA), 2:(new series)4 October 1966, pp. 735-877.
Rare Book Room PS3511.R94 Z9173 1966

"Robert Frost in England," in *The Courier* (Syracuse, NY), No. 30 (Fall 1968), pp. 5-6.
Rare Book Room PS3511.R94 Z9163

Robert Frost: Lectures on the Centennial of His Birth.
Washington: Library of Congress, 1975.
Lectures delivered by Helen Bacon, Peter Davison, Robert Pack, and Allen Tate at a symposium held March 26, 1974 in the Library of Congress under the auspices of the Gertrude Clarke Whittall Poetry and Literature Fund.
Rare Book Room PS3511.R94 Z917 (3 copies)

Robert Frost New Hampshire.
Compiled by William B. Ewert, with a biobibliography by Barbara Hodgdon.
Durham, NH: Friends of the Library, Univ. of New Hampshire, 1976.
Catalog of resources found in the William B. Ewert-Robert Frost Collection of the University of New Hampshire Library and the George H. Browne-Robert Frost Collection of the Plymouth State College Library.
Rare Book Room PS3511.R94 Z69 1976 (2 copies)

Robert Frost: The Critical Reception.
Edited with an introduction by Linda W. Wagner.
[New York]: Burt Franklin & Co., c1977.
Rare Book Room PS3511.R94 Z9185 1977

Robert Frost: The Man and His Work.
New York: Henry Holt and Company, [1923]
Includes contributions by Amy Lowell, Louis Untermeyer and Percy H. Boynton.
Rare Book Room PS3511.R94 Z9188 1923

Rotella, Guy L.
Reading & Writing Nature: The Poetry of Robert Frost, Wallace Stevens, Marianne Moore, and Elizabeth Bishop.
Boston: Northeastern University Press, c1991.
Dust jacket.
Rare Book Room PS310.N3 R68 1991 (2 copies)

Sergeant, Elizabeth Shepley.
Fire Under the Andes; a Group of North American Portraits.
New York: Alfred A. Knopf, 1927.
Includes a chapter on Robert Frost, pp. 285-303.
Rare Book Room E176 .S48

Sergeant, Elizabeth Shepley.
Robert Frost; the Trial By Existence.
New York: Holt, Rinehart and Winston, c1960.
First edition. Dust jacket.
Rare Book Room PS3511.R94 Z92 c.2

 Sergeant, Howard.
Tradition in the Making of Modern Poetry, Volume 1.
London: Britannicus Liber Limited, 1951.
Includes commentary on Robert Frost, pp. 78-84. Dust jacket.
Rare Book Room PR601.S4 v.1

Seven Gables Bookshop.
More First Books by American Authors, 1727 to 1977.
New York: Seven Gables Bookshop, Inc., c1972.
Rare Book Room PS504 .S48 1972

Smythe, Daniel.
Robert Frost Speaks.
New York: Twayne Publishers, Inc., c1964.
"Recreation of the setting and the atmosphere of the author's interviews with Mr. Frost into which much of their conversations are woven." Copy 1 is inscribed to Frank Piskor by the author.
Rare Book Room PS3511.R94 Z924 c.2

Smythe, Daniel.
Visits With Robert Frost.
Francestown, NH: Golden Quill Press, c1974.
Copies 1 and 2 are signed by author.
Rare Book Room PS3511.R94 Z924 1974 (2 copies)

Snow, Wilbert.
Codline's Child; the Autobiography of Wilbert Snow.
Middletown, CT: Wesleyan University Press, c1974.
First edition. Includes a chapter on Robert Frost, pp. 346-384. Library's copy has inscription to Frank Piskor by the author. Dust jacket.
Rare Book Room PS3537.N683 Z5

Southworth, James G.
Some Modern American Poets.
Oxford: Basil Blackwell, 1950.
Includes chapters on Robert Frost, pp. [42]-87. Dust jacket.
Rare Book Room PS305 .S58

Squire, J. C.
Contemporary American Authors.
Introduction by Henry Seidel Canby.
New York: Henry Holt and Company, c1928.
A chapter on Robert Frost on pp. 15-42.
Rare Book Room PS221 .S7

Squires, Radcliffe.
The Major Themes of Robert Frost.
Ann Arbor: University of Michigan Press, c1963.
Dust jacket.
Rare Book Room PS3511.R94 Z925 c.2

Stegner, Wallace.
The Uneasy Chair; a Biography of Bernard DeVoto.
Garden City, NY: Doubleday & Company, Inc., 1974.
First edition. Includes several pages of commentary on Robert Frost. Dust jacket.
Rare Book Room PS3507.E867 Z9 c.2

Sutton, Walter.
Ezra Pound, a Collection of Critical Essays.
Englewood Cliffs, NJ: Prentice-Hall, Inc., c1963.
Twentieth century views. Copy 3 has inscription to Frank Piskor by the author.
Rare Book Room PS3531.O82 Z85 c.3

Tatham, David.
A Poet Recognized:
Notes About Robert Frost's First Trip to England and Where He Lived.
Drawings by Vaughn Bode.
[n.p.], 1969.
"This first printing is limited to 200 copies." Copy 1 has inscription by author.
Rare Book Room PS3511.R94 Z9268 1969 (5 copies)

Tatham, David.
Robert Frost's White Mountains.
Worcester, MA: Achille J. St. Onge, 1974.
Limited to 500 copies. Library's copy has inscription by author.
Rare Book Room PS3511.R94 Z929 1974

Thompson, Lawrance.
"An Early Frost Broadside," in *The New Colophon: A Book Collectors' Quarterly* (New York), 1:part 1, January 1948, pp. 5-12.
Rare Book Room PS3511.R94 Z929 1948

Thompson, Lawrance.
Fire and Ice: The Art and Thought of Robert Frost.
New York: Henry Holt and Company, 1942.
Library's copy has inscription to Frank Piskor by the author. Dust jacket.
Rare Book Room PS3511.R94 Z93

Thompson, Lawrance.
Robert Frost: The Early Years, 1874-1915.
New York: Holt, Rinehart and Winston, c1966.
First edition. Dust jacket.
Rare Book Room PS3511.R94 Z953 v.1 c.2

Thompson, Lawrance and Winnick, R. H.
Robert Frost: The Later Years, 1938-1963.
New York: Holt, Rinehart and Winston, c1976.
First edition. Dust jacket.
Rare Book Room PS3511.R94 Z953 v.3 c.2

Thompson, Lawrance.
Robert Frost: The Years of Triumph, 1915-1938.
New York: Holt, Rinehart and Winston, c1970.
First edition. Dust jacket.
Rare Book Room PS3511.R94 Z953 v.2 c.2

Thompson, Lawrance.
Robert Frost.
Minneapolis: University of Minnesota Press, c1959.
University of Minnesota pamphlets on American writers; no. 2. Library's copy has inscription to Frank Piskor by the author.
Rare Book Room PS3511.R94 Z95 1959

Thompson, Lawrance. and Winnick, R. H.
Robert Frost, a Biography.
New York: Holt, Rinehart and Winston, 1982, c1981.
First edition. "The authorized life of the poet condensed into a single volume edited by Edward Connery Lathem." Dust jacket.
Rare Book Room PS3511.R94 Z954 1982

Tres escritores norteamericanos: Ernest Hemingway; William Faulkner; Robert Frost.
Madrid: Editorial Gredos, 1961.
Spanish edition. Originally published as University of Minnesota Pamphlets on American Writers, nos.1-3.
Rare Book Room PS379 .T7 1961

Untermeyer, Jean Starr.
Private Collection.
New York: Alfred A. Knopf, 1965.
First edition. Includes commentary on Robert Frost. Dust jacket.
Rare Book Room PS3541.N715 Z5 1965

Untermeyer, Louis.
Bygones: The Recollections of Louis Untermeyer.
New York: Harcourt, Brace & World, c1965.
Includes a chapter about Robert Frost on pp. [44]-51. Dust jacket.
Rare Book Room PS3541.N72 Z52 1965

Untermeyer, Louis.
From Another World; the Autobiography of Louis Untermeyer.
New York: Harcourt, Brace and Company, c1939.
First edition. Includes commentary on Robert Frost. Dust jacket.
Rare Book Room PS3541.N72 Z5 c.2

 Untermeyer, Louis.
These Times.
New York: Henry Holt and Company, 1917.
Dedicated to Robert Frost. Poems, reprinted in part from various periodicals.
Rare Book Room PS3541.N72 T5 1917

Van Doren, Carl.
Three Worlds.
New York: Harper & Brothers, 1936.
First edition. Includes commentaries on Robert Frost.
Rare Book Room PS3543.A555 Z5 1936

Van Doren, Mark.
Introduction to Poetry; Commentaries on Thirty Poems.
New York: Hill and Wang, 1968.
Rare Book Room PR1175 .V23 1968 c.2

Van Doren, Mark.
Three Plays.
New York: Hill and Wang, c1966.
First edition. Library's copy is inscribed to Frank Piskor by author. Dust jacket.
Rare Book Room PS3543.A557 A19 1966

Van Egmond, Peter.
Robert Frost: A Reference Guide, 1974-1990.
Boston, MA: G. K. Hall & Co., c1991.
Rare Book Room PS3511.R94 Z549 1991

Von Dreele, W. H.
If Liberals Had Feathers ... Gee: What a Hunter I Would Be:
A Collection of Libertarian Advice and Comment.
Illustrated by Mary Gauerke; foreword by William F. Buckley, Jr.
New York: Devin-Adair Company, c1967.
Library's copy is signed by Von Dreele with a letter to Frank Piskor from David Tatham who received it from Lesley Frost Ballantine, March 4, 1968.
Rare Book Room PN6162 .V6 1967

Waggoner, Hyatt Howe.
The Heel of Elohim: Science and Values in Modern American Poetry.
Norman: University of Oklahoma Press, c1950.
Includes chapter on Robert Frost on pp. 41-60. Dust jacket.
Rare Book Room PS324.W3 c.2

Walsh, John Evangelist.
Into My Own: The English Years of Robert Frost, 1912-1915.
New York: Grove Press, c1988.
First edition. Dust jacket.
Rare Book Room PS3511.R94 Z985 1988 c.2

Wesleyan University Library.
Robert Frost: A Chronological Survey Compiled in Connection With an Exhibit of His Work at the Olin Memorial Library, Wesleyan University, April 1936.
Compiled by L. R. Thompson.
Limited to 250 numbered copies. Library's copy is number 64.
Rare Book Room PS3511.R94 Z986 1936

West, Herbert Faulkner.
The Mind on the Wing: A Book for Readers and Collectors.
New York: Coward-McCann, Inc., [c1947]
Includes references to Robert Frost. Library's copy has inscription to Frank Piskor by the author. Dust jacket.
Rare Book Room PN511 .W4 1947

Whicher, George Frisbie.
"[Letter about Robert Frost to "The Crow's Nest: Observations by the Ordinary Seaman" section] in *The Colophon, New Series: A Quarterly for Bookmen* (New York), 2:4, Autumn 1937, pp. 617-618.
Rare Book Room PS3511.R94 Z987

Whicher, George Frisbie.
Poetry and Civilization; Essays.
Collected and edited by Harriet Fox Whicher.
Ithaca, NY: Published for Amherst College by Cornell University Press, c1955.
"The writings of George Frisbie Whicher": pp. 141-142. Includes chapter "Out for stars: A meditation on Robert Frost" on pp. 19-30.
Rare Book Room PS121 .W47 1955

[84] *The Writer and His Craft.*
Foreword by Roy W. Cowden.
Ann Arbor: University of Michigan Press, 1956.
First edition as an Ann Arbor paperback, third printing. The Hopwood lectures for 1932-1952, by Robert Morss Lovett and others. Includes "The Themes of Robert Frost" by Robert Penn Warren (pp. 218-233).

Writers at Work: The Paris Review Interviews, Second Series.
Prepared for book publication by George Plimpton; introduced by Van Wyck Brooks.
New York: Viking Press, c1963.
Includes chapter about Robert Frost on pp. [7]-34. Dust jacket.

FROST CHRISTMAS CARDS

Two Tramps in Mud Time: A New Poem.
New York: Spiral Press, 1934.
Library's part 1 has inscription by the author. Library's part 1 issued as holiday greetings from Ann & Joseph Blumenthal, December 1934. Library's part 2 issued as holiday greetings from the Melchers, December 1934.
Rare Book Room PS3511.R94 A6c 1934 (2 parts)

Neither Out Far Nor in Deep.
New York: Spiral Press, c1935.
Library's part 1 issued as holiday greetings from Elinor & Robert Frost, December 1935. Library's part 2 issued as holiday greetings from the Melchers, December 1935. Library's part 3 issued as holiday greetings from Ann & Joseph Blumenthal, December 1935.
Rare Book Room PS3511.R94 A6c 1935 (3 parts)

From Snow to Snow.
New York: Henry Holt, c1936.
Second printing from the first edition plates was used by Frost as the Christmas greeting for 1936.

To a Young Wretch.
New York: Spiral Press, 1937.
Library's part 1 issued as holiday greetings from Elinor and Robert Frost, December 1937. Library's part 2 issued as holiday greetings from the Melchers, December 1937.
Rare Book Room PS3511.R94 A6c 1937 (2 parts)

Carpe Diem.
[n.p.], 1938.
Library's part 1 is signed by the author. Library's part 1 issued as holiday greetings from T. J. Wilson.
Rare Book Room PS3511.R94 A6c 1938 (1 part)

Triple Plate.
New York: Spiral Press, c1939.
Library's part 1 issued as holiday greetings from Robert Frost, December 1939. Library's part 2 issued as holiday greetings from the Melchers, December 1939. Library's part 3 issued as holiday greetings from Henry Holt and Company, December 1939.
Rare Book Room PS3511.R94 A6c 1939 (3 parts)

Our Hold on the Planet.
[n.p.], c1940.
Library's part 1 issued as holiday greetings from Marguerite and Fred Melcher, December 1940.
Rare Book Room PS3511.R94 A6c 1940 (1 part)

I Could Give All to Time.
[n.p.], c1941.
Library's part 1 has inscription by the author. Library's part 1 issued as holiday greetings from Henry Holt and Company, December 1941.
Rare Book Room PS3511.R94 A6c 1941 (1 part)

The Gift Outright.
[n.p.], 1942.
Library's part 1 issued as holiday greetings from Henry Holt and Company, December 1942.
Rare Book Room PS3511.R94 A6c 1942 (1 part)

The Guardeen.
Los Angeles: Ward Ritchie Press, 1943.
Limited to 96 copies. Library's copy is number 15. Issued as holiday greetings from Earle J. Bernheimer, Christmas 1943, signed by him.
Rare Book Room PS3511.R94 A6b 1943

Two Leading Lights.
Los Angeles: Ward Ritchie Press, 1944.
Limited to 52 copies. Library's copy is number 15. Issued as holiday greetings from Earle J. Bernheimer, Christmas 1944, signed by him.
Rare Book Room PS3511.R94 A6b 1944

An Unstamped Letter in Our Rural Letter Box.
New York: Spiral Press, c1944.
Library's part 1 issued as holiday greetings from Ann & Joseph Blumenthal, December 1944. Library's part 2 issued as holiday greetings from Henry Holt and Company, December 1944.
Rare Book Room PS3511.R94 A6c 1944 (2 parts)

On Making Certain Anything Has Happened.
New York: Spiral Press, 1945.
Library's part 1 issued as holiday greetings from Joseph A. Brandt, December 1945. Library's part 2 issued as holiday greetings from Marguerite & Fred Melcher, December 1945.
Rare Book Room PS3511.R94 A6c 1945 (2 parts, 2 copies of part 1)

A Young Birch.
New York: Spiral Press, 1946.
Library's part 1 issued as holiday greetings from Henry Holt & Company, December 1946. Library's part 2 issued as holiday greetings from Joseph A. Brandt, December 1946.
Rare Book Room PS3511.R94 A6c 1946 (2 parts)

The Falls.
Los Angeles: Ward Ritchie Press, 1947.
Limited to 60 copies. Library's copy is number 16. Issued as holiday greetings from Earle J. Bernheimer, Christmas 1947, signed by him.
Rare Book Room PS3511.R94 A6b 1947

One Step Backward Taken.
New York: Spiral Press, 1947.
Library's part 1 issued as holiday greetings from Robert Frost, December 1947. Library's part 2 issued as holiday greetings from Mr. & Mrs. Joseph A. Brandt, December 1947.
Rare Book Room PS3511.R94 A6c 1947 (2 parts, 2 copies of each)

Closed For Good.
New York: Spiral Press, 1948.
Library's part 1 issued as holiday greetings from Robert Frost, December 1948. Library's part 2 issued as holiday greetings from Alfred C. Edwards, December 1948.
Rare Book Room PS3511.R94 A6c 1948 (2 parts)

 On the Inflation of the Currency.
[United States: Earle J. Bernheimer, 1948]
Limited to 60 copies. Library's copy is number 15. Issued as holiday greetings from Earle J. Bernheimer, Christmas 1948, signed by him.
Rare Book Room PS3511.R94 A6b 1948

On a Tree Fallen Across the Road (To Hear Us Talk).
New York: Spiral Press, 1949.
Library's part 1 issued as holiday greetings from Robert Frost, December 1949. Library's part 2 issued as holiday greetings from Lesley & Robert Frost, December 1949. Library's part 3 issued as holiday greetings from Henry Holt & Company, December 1949. Library's part 1 has inscription by Lesley Frost.
Rare Book Room PS3511.R94 A6c 1949 (3 parts)

Doom to Bloom.
New York: Spiral Press, 1950.
Library's part 1 issued as holiday greetings from Lesley Frost, December 1950. Library's part 2 issued as holiday greetings from Lesley and Robert Frost, December 1950. Library's part 3 issued as holiday greetings from Ann & Joseph Blumenthal, December 1950. Library's part 1 is signed by Lesley Frost and part 2 is inscribed by Lesley Frost.
Rare Book Room PS3511.R94 A6c 1950 (3 parts, 2 copies of part 2)

A Cabin in the Clearing.
New York: Spiral Press, 1951.
Library's part 1 has no greeting information. Library's part 2 issued as holiday greetings from Henry Holt and Company, December 1951.
Rare Book Room PS3511.R94 A6c 1951 (2 parts)

Does No One But Me At All Ever Feel This Way In the Least.
New York: Spiral Press, 1952.
Library's part 1 issued as holiday greetings from Lesley Frost, December 1952. Library's part 2 issued as holiday greetings from Marguerite and Fred Melcher, December 1952. Library's part 3 issued as holiday greetings from Alfred C. Edwards, December 1952. Library's part 1 is signed by Lesley Frost.
Rare Book Room PS3511.R94 A6c 1952 (3 parts)

One More Brevity: A New Poem..
New York: Spiral Press, c1953.

Library's part 1 issued as holiday greetings from Lesley Frost, December 1953. Library's part 2 issued as holiday greetings from Marguerite & Fred Melcher, December 1953. Library's part 3 issued as holiday greetings from Henry Holt and Company, December 1953. Library's part 1, copies 1 and 2, are both signed by Lesley Frost.

Rare Book Room PS3511.R94 A6c 1953 (3 parts, 2 copies of part 1)

FROM A MILKWEED POD

BY ROBERT FROST

A new poem by Robert Frost

at Christmas 1954 again comes

to you with warm greetings for

the holidays from

Lesley Frost and Joseph W. Ballantine

From a Milkweed Pod.
New York: Spiral Press, 1954.

Library's part 1 issued as holiday greetings from Lesley Frost, December 1954. Library's part 2 issued as holiday greetings from Marguerite and Fred Melcher, December 1954. Library's part 1, copies 1 and 3 are inscribed by Lesley Frost. Library's part 1, copy 2 is signed by Lesley Frost.

Rare Book Room PS3511.R94 A6c 1954 (2 parts, 3 copies of part 1)

Some Science Fiction.
New York: Spiral Press, c1955.

Library's part 1 issued as holiday greetings from Lesley Frost and Joseph W. Ballantine, December 1955. Library's part 2 issued as holiday greetings from Al Edwards, December 1955. Library's part 3 issued as holiday greetings from

Henry Holt and Company, December 1955.
Rare Book Room PS3511.R94 A6c 1955 (3 parts, 2 copies of part 1)

Kitty Hawk: 1894.
New York: Spiral Press, 1956.
Library's part 1 issued as holiday greetings from Robert Frost, December 1956. Library's part 2 issued as holiday greetings from Henry Holt and Company, December 1954. Library's part 3 issued as holiday greetings from Marguerite and Fred Melcher, December 1954. Library's part 4 issued as holiday greetings from Phyllis and William Prescott Frost, December 1954.
Rare Book Room PS3511.R94 A6c 1956 (4 parts, 2 copies of part 1)

My Objection to Being Stepped On.
New York: Spiral Press, 1957.
Library's copy of part 1-11 issued as holiday greetings, December 1957, and are enclosed in protective case. Library's part 1 copy 1 has inscription and corrections of title by author.
Rare Book Room PS3511.R94 A6c 1957

Away.
New York: Spiral Press, 1958.
Library's part 1 issued as holiday greetings from Lesley Frost, December 1958. Library's part 2 issued as holiday greetings from Robert Frost, December 1958. Library's part 3 issued as holiday greetings from Marguerite and Fred Melcher, December 1958. Library's part 1, copy 1 is signed by Lesley Frost. Library's part 2, copies 2 and 3 have inscriptions by the author.
Rare Book Room PS3511.R94 A6c 1958 (3 parts, 2 copies of part 1, 3 copies of part 2)

A-Wishing Well.
New York: Spiral Press, 1959.
Library's part 1 issued as holiday greetings from Robert Frost, December 1959. Library's part 2 issued as holiday greetings from Lesley Frost Ballantine and Joseph W. Ballantine, December 1959. Library's part 3 issued as holiday greetings from Marguerite and Fred Melcher, December 1959.
Rare Book Room PS3511.R94 A6c 1959 (3 parts, 2 copies of parts 1 and 2 each)

Accidentally on Purpose.
New York: Spiral Press, 1960.
Library's part 1 issued as holiday greetings from Robert Frost, December 1960.

Library's part 2 issued as holiday greetings from Marguerite and Fred Melcher, December 1960. Library's part 3 issued as holiday greetings from Lesley Frost Ballantine and Joseph W. Ballantine, December 1960. Library's part 3, copy 1 is signed by Lesley Frost.

Rare Book Room PS3511.R94 A6c 1960 (3 parts, 3 copies of part 1)

Accidentally on Purpose.
New York: Spiral Press, 1960

A complete set of twenty imprints, inscribed "To Frank Piskor/twenty volumes complete/from as always/Robert Frost." In leather clamshell box.

Rare Book Room PS3511.R94 A6c 1960

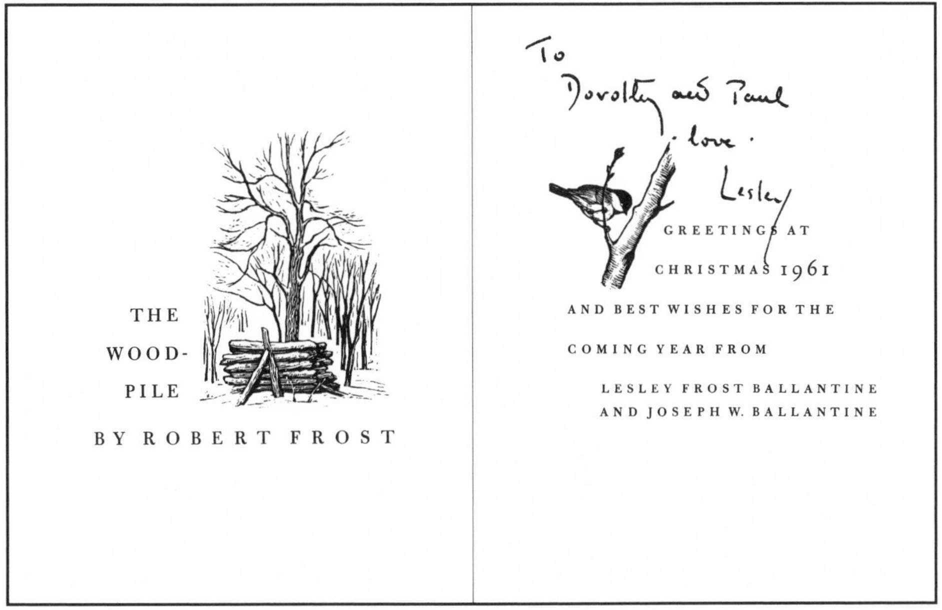

The Wood-Pile.
New York: Spiral Press, 1961.

Library's part 1 issued as holiday greetings from Lesley & Stanislav Zimic, December 1961. Library's part 2 issued as holiday greetings from Lesley Frost Ballantine and Joseph W. Ballantine, December 1961. Library's part 3 issued as holiday greetings from Robert Frost, December 1961. Library's part 2, copy 1 is signed by Lesley Frost Ballantine. Library's part 2, copy 3 is signed by Lesley Frost.

Rare Book Room PS3511.R94 A6c 1961 (3 parts, 3 copies of part 2)

The Prophets Really Prophesy as Mystics, the Commentators Merely by Statistics: A New Poem.
New York: Spiral Press, 1962.
Library's part 1 issued as holiday greetings from Robert Frost, December 1962.
Library's part 2 issued as holiday greetings from Holt, Rinehart and Winston, December 1962.
Rare Book Room PS3511.R94 A6c 1962 (2 parts, 2 copies of part 1, 3 copies of part 2)

The Constant Symbol.
[S.l.: s.n., 1962 (New York: Spiral Press)]
Issued as holiday greetings from Cornelia & Waller Barrett, Christmas 1962.
Rare Book Room PS3511.R94 A6c 1962b (2 copies)

New Hampshire Historical Society.
Holiday Greetings From Robert Frost.
[Somersworth, NH: New Hampshire Publishing Co.], 1971.
A loan exhibit held at the New Hampshire Historical Society, Concord, December 1971. 750 copies of this keepsake were designed and printed for the New Hampshire Publishing Company, Somersworth.
Rare Book Room PS3511.R94 A6a 1971 (3 copies)

WORKS BY PHILIP BOOTH

New England poet Philip Booth (1925-) was a close friend of Frost's in his later years and a writer in whom Frost took considerable interest. Dr. Piskor knew Booth at Syracuse University in the early sixties and collected his work along with Frost's.

Available Light.
New York: Viking Press, c1976.
Library's copy includes inscription to Frank Piskor by the author. Dust jacket.
Rare Book Room PS3552.O647 A95 1976

Before Sleep.
New York: The Viking Press, c1980.
Library's copy includes inscription to Frank Piskor by the author. Dust jacket.
Rare Book Room PS3552.O647 B4 1980 (2 copies)

Beyond Our Fears: Prayers For Today.
[S.l.: s.n.]; New York: [Distributed by] St. George's Episcopal Church, [197?]
Library's copy includes inscription to Frank Piskor by the author.
Rare Book Room BV260.B488

The Islanders.
New York: The Viking Press, 1961.
Both copies are inscribed by the author. Both copies in dust jacket.
Rare Book Room PS3552.O647 I8 (2 copies)

Ladd, Gabrielle.
The Dark Island: Twenty Poems.
Lunenburg, VT: The Stinehour Press, c1960.
Library's copy is inscribed to Frank Piskor by P[hilip] B[ooth].
Rare Book Room PS3523.A253 D3 1960

[94] *Letter From a Distant Land.*
New York: The Viking Press, 1957.
Both copies are inscribed by the author. Both copies in dust jacket.
Rare Book Room PS3552.O647 L4 (2 copies)

Margins: a Sequence of New and Selected Poems.
New York: The Viking Press, c1970.
Library's copy 1 inscribed to Frank Piskor by the author. Both copies in dust jacket.
Rare Book Room PS3552.O647 M3 1970 (2 copies)

Relations: Selected Poems, 1950-1985.
New York: Penguin Books, c1986.
Rare Book Room PS3552.O647 R4 1986b

Weathers and Edges.
New York: The Viking Press, c1966.
Library's copy is inscribed to Frank Piskor by the author. Dust jacket.
Rare Book Room PS3552.O647 W4 1966

Stone

That Baltimore Jesus, his doctoring arms
outstretched to the sick at Johns Hopkins,
weighted on me in that last of waiting rooms.
I tried to belive I was one of his sons.

Come unto me was his hand's burden, all ye
that are heavy laden, and I will give you rest.
But stone could not come to me; nor I
to stone, with stone thick in my chest.

Philip Booth
Thanksgiving 1953 - December 1957

This holograph is for Frank Piskor, a poet
among administrators, who administers
to poets with a care that makes humanity of stone.

WORKS BY EDWARD AND HELEN THOMAS

The English poet Edward Thomas (1878-1917) was an early friend of Frost's during his England years and was collected by Dr. Piskor along with Frost. The two poets were very close and Frost's eulogy "To E. T." is a tribute to his friend, who died in action in World War I.

Bodleian Library
Edward Thomas, 1878-1917:
An Exhibition Held in the Divinity School, Oxford, 1968.
Oxford, Eng.: Bodleian Library, 1968.
Rare Book Room PR6039.H55 Z77 1968

Cooke, William.
Edward Thomas: A Critical Biography, 1878-1917.
London: Faber and Faber, 1970.
Includes a bibliography of Edward Thomas's published works (pp. 279-287). Dust jacket. Several references to Robert Frost.
Rare Book Room PR6039.H55 Z65 1970

Eckert, Robert P.
Edward Thomas: A Biography and a Bibliography.
London: J. M. Dent & Sons Ltd., 1937.
Extensive bibliography on the works of Edward Thomas (pp. 185-288). Dust jacket. Several references to Robert Frost.
Rare Book Room PR6039.H55 Z7 1937

Farjeon, Eleanor.
Edward Thomas: The Last Four Years. Book One of the Memoirs of Eleanor Farjeon.
London: Oxford University Press, 1958.
Dust jacket. Several references to Robert Frost.
Rare Book Room PR6039.H55 Z484 1958

Moore, John.
The Life and Letters of Edward Thomas.
London; Toronto: William Heinemann Ltd., 1939.
Several references to Robert Frost.
Rare Book Room PR6039.H55 Z76 1939

Oxford.
Painted by John Fulleylove, R. I.
London: A. & C. Black, 1903.
First edition. Limited to 300 numbered copies. Library's copy is number 277.
Rare Book Room PR6039.T45 1903

Scannell, Vernon.
Edward Thomas.
[London]: Longmans, Green & Co., c1963.
Published for The British Council and the National Book League. Writers and Their Work: No. 163.
Rare Book Room PR6039.H55 Z79 1963

Thomas, Edward. Eckert 193
Beautiful Wales.
Painted by Robert Fowler; described by Edward Thomas with a note on Mr. Fowler's landscapes by Alex J. Finberg.
London: A. & C. Black, 1905.
First edition. Binding: dark green cloth. Front cover bordered by double olive-green rule, then divided by rules with red berries into six panels, three shorter at top, the center lettered in gilt. Spine bordered by double olive-green rule, lettered in gilt. Back cover blank. Endpapers white. Top edge gilt, fore-edge untrimmed, bottom edge trimmed. Republished in part from *Daily Chronicle, the World, the Week's Survey, the Outlook,* and *the Illustrated London News.*
Rare Book Room DA730 .T45 1905

Thomas, Edward. Eckert 246-247
Collected Poems.
Foreword by Walter de la Mare.
London: Selwyn and Blount, Ltd., 1920.
First edition. Binding: blue cloth. Front cover blank, spine with white paper

label bordered by thick and thin line, lettered in black, back cover blank.
Endpapers white. Top edge trimmed, fore and bottom edges untrimmed.
Rare Book Room PR6039.H55 A17 1920

Thomas, Edward. Eckert 228-229
The Country.
London: B. T. Batsford, 1913.
First edition. Binding: blue cloth. Front cover with ornamental border in gilt enclosing panel formed by broken and whole rule, lettered in gilt. Spine bordered by single rule in gilt, curved top and bottom, lettered in gilt. Back cover bears publisher's monogram stamped in gilt. Top edge gilt, fore and bottom edges untrimmed.
Rare Book Room PR6039.H55 C6 1913

Thomas, Edward. Eckert 206-207
Feminine Influence on the Poets.
London: Martin Secker, 1910.
First edition. Binding: light blue cloth. Front cover bordered by double blind rule, lettered in gilt with three panels formed by two vertical double rules and top of two outer panels bordered by single rule, within center panel. Spine bordered by double blind rule, stamped in gilt. Back cover blank. End-papers white. Top edge trimmed and stained blue. Fore and bottom edges untrimmed.
Rare Book Room PN56.W7 T6 1910b

Thomas, Edward. Eckert 226-227
The Icknield Way.
Illustrations by A. L. Collins.
London: Constable & Company Ltd., 1913.
First edition, second issue. Binding: green ribbed cloth. Front cover bordered by blind rule enclosing a panel with illustration in gilt, and the title in gilt. Spine stamped in gilt, back cover bordered with blind rule. Endpapers white. Top edge trimmed, fore and bottom edges untrimmed.
Rare Book Room DA630 .T6123 1913

[98] 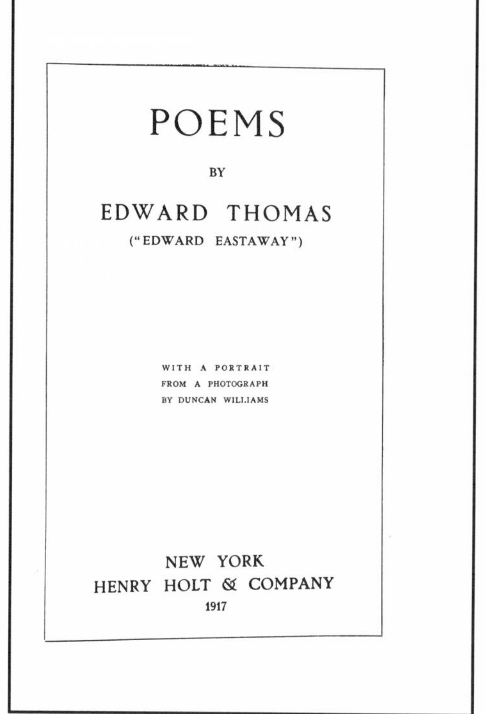

POEMS

BY

EDWARD THOMAS

("EDWARD EASTAWAY")

WITH A PORTRAIT
FROM A PHOTOGRAPH
BY DUNCAN WILLIAMS

NEW YORK
HENRY HOLT & COMPANY
1917

Thomas, Edward. *Poems*.
New York: Henry Holt, 1917.

Thomas, Edward. Eckert 232-233
In Pursuit of Spring.
London; New York: Thomas Nelson and Sons, 1914.

First edition. Binding: blue ribbed cloth. Front cover bordered by double light blue rule, lettered in gilt. Spine bordered by double light blue rule, lettered in gilt. Back cover blank. Endpapers gray-green. Map on lining papers. Top edge gilt, fore and bottom edges untrimmed.

Rare Book Room PR6039.H55 Z467 1914

Thomas, Edward. Eckert 244
Poems.
New York: Henry Holt & Company, 1917.

First American edition. Binding: blue paper covered boards with dark blue cloth backstrip. Front cover with panel formed by double rules in black, lettered in black. Spine with blue paper label lettered in black from top to bottom. Back cover blank. Endpapers white. All edges trimmed. With a portrait from a photograph by Duncan Williams. Dedicated to Robert Frost.

Rare Book Room PR6039.H55 A17 1917

SELECTED POEMS
of Edward Thomas

With an Introduction by
Edward Garnett

THE GREGYNOG PRESS
MCMXXVII

Thomas, Edward.
Selected Poems.
Newtown, Wales:
Gregynog Press, 1927.
Frost and Thomas were close friends until the latter's untimely death in World War I. Gregynog books are highly valued.

Thomas, Edward. Eckert 255-256
Selected Poems of Edward Thomas.
Introduction by Edward Garnett.
[Newtown, Montgomeryshire]: The Gregynog Press, 1927.

First edition, second state. Limited to 275 numbered copies. Library's copy is number 216. Binding: yellow buckram. Front cover blank, spine lettered in gilt, back cover blank. Endpapers Japanese vellum. All edges trimmed.

Rare Book Room PR6039.H55 A17 1927

[100] Thomas, Edward. Eckert 201-202

The South Country.

London: J. M. Dent and Co., 1909.

First edition. Binding: pale green cloth. Front cover bordered by greenish-brown rule broken by circles and at each corner by heart, enclosing, on either side, from top to bottom, a rose, a heart, a rose, a heart, and a rose. Between roses at bottom, a heart. Title stamped in gilt. Spine stamped in gilt, back cover blank. Endpapers, ploughing scene green on white. All edges trimmed. Heart of England series.

Rare Book Room QH81 .T37 1909

Thomas, Helen.

As It Was.

New York: Harper & Brothers, 1927.

Rare Book Room PR6039.H55 Z85 1927a

Thomas, Helen.

As It Was: And World Without End.

London: Faber and Faber, 1956.

"As It Was" first published in 1926 by William Heinemann Limited; "World Without End" first published in 1931 by William Heinemann Limited". Dust jacket.

Rare Book Room PR6039.H55 Z85 1956

Abbreviations used in this listing:
EWF = Elinor White Frost
LFB = Lesley Frost Ballantine
FPP = Frank Peter Piskor

I. Material by Frost

A. Correspondence
[Arranged alphabetically by correspondent]

Sylvester Baxter
1923. Frost to Baxter. reprinted in R. C. Townsend's "In Defense of Form: A Letter from Robert Frost to Sylvester Baxter, 1923," *New England Quarterly*. June 1963. pp. 241-249.

Philip Booth
1963. January 10. Frost to Booth. dictated to Mrs. Chisholm Gentry. photocopy. Accompanying note from Mrs. Gentry to Booth.
[n.d.] Booth's reply to above. photocopy.

W. S. Braithwaite
1958. August 11. Frost to Braithwaite. Ripton VT. photocopy.

Dean Briggs
1897. September 11. Frost to Dean Briggs [of Harvard]. Lawrence MA. reprinted in *Harvard Alumni Bulletin*. February 12, 1955. pp. 346-348.

Stuart Gerry Brown
1952. September 19. Frost to Brown. Ripton VT. photocopy and transcript of original. Accompanying obituary for Brown and two offprints of the article on John Jay Chapman mentioned in the letter.

Robert Chase
1952. March 4. Frost to Chase. South Miami FL. photocopy. [Note by FPP: an important letter.]

 Dorothy Cleaveland

1951. March 17. Frost to Cleaveland. Cambridge MA. als. [Note: this letter is not part of the Piskor collection; it is listed here for the convenience of scholars. It is located in Miscellaneous Manuscripts under "Frost."]

Mildred Flagg

1958. October 28. Mildred Flagg to Frost. Newtonville MA. carbon copy of tl.

1959. March 24. Frost to Flagg. Cambridge MA. als. Accompanying letters to Frost and Flagg from Donald Miller.

Lesley Frost

1917. September 26. Frost to Lesley. Franconia NH. carbon copy of tls. Inscription by LFB to FPP.

[Henry Holt and Company]

1946. July 19. Frost to Dear Helen. Ripton VT. printed transcript from autograph dealer's catalog.

1944-1946. 34 letters relating to publication of the Modern Library edition of Frost's poems, *The Pocket Book of Robert Frost* and *The Constant Symbol.* Also includes the contract form for *The Constant Symbol.*

Robert Hillyer

All carbon copies of transcripts accompanied by letter from Gail Gager. All photocopies of originals accompanied by carbon copy of a memorandum from Martin Bush to David Fraser.

1923. January 25. Frost to Hillyer. South Shaftsbury VT. carbon copy of transcript.

1924. March 12. Frost to Hillyer. Amherst MA. carbon copy of transcript.

1924. July 26. Frost to Hillyer. Amherst MA. carbon copy of transcript.

1931. February 4. Frost to Hillyer. Amherst MA. carbon copy of transcript.

1932. September 28. Frost to Hillyer. Monrovia CA. carbon copy of transcript.

1934. September 5. Frost to Hillyer. Franconia NH. carbon copy of transcript.

1935. March 23. Frost to Hillyer. Key West FL. carbon copy of transcript.

1937. September 15. Frost to Hillyer. Concord Corners VT. carbon copy of transcript.

1937. February 9. Frost to Hillyer. San Antonio TX. carbon copy of transcript.
1937. June 16. Frost to Hillyer. South Shaftsbury VT. carbon copy of transcript.
1938. April 14. Frost to Hillyer. Gainesville FL. photocopy of original and carbon copy of transcript.
1938. April 20. Frost to Hillyer. photocopy of telegram.
1938. July 20. Frost to Hillyer. South Shaftsbury VT. carbon copy of transcript.
1938. August 11. Frost to Hillyer. South Shaftsbury VT. carbon copy of transcript.
1949. [December]. Frost to Hillyer. photocopy of note on Christmas card.
1953. November 20. Frost to Hillyer. New Ark of the Covenant. photocopy.
1959. February 20. Frost to Hillyer. South Miami FL. photcopy.
1961. January 1. Frost to Hillyer. Cambridge MA. photocopy.

Edward Morgan Lewis

Given to FPP by Dr. Applegate. Accompanying letter from Andree D. Hest.

1925. February 28. Frost to Lewis. Amherst MA. photocopy.
1933. July 28. Frost to Lewis. South Shaftsbury VT. photocopy.
1933. August 14. Frost to Lewis. South Shaftsbury VT. photocopy.

Given to FPP by David Tatham. Accompanying letter from David Tatham enclosing a letter from Bruce Catton to Tatham concerning Frost.

1925. February 28. Frost to Lewis. Amherst MA. photocopy and typed transcription.
1925. February 28. Frost to Lewis. Amherst MA. typed transcription.
1930. June 23. Frost to Lewis. South Shaftsbury MA. photocopy.
1933. July 28. Frost to Lewis. South Shaftsbury VT. photocopy and typed transcription.
1933 August 14. Frost to Lewis. South Shaftsbury VT. photocopy.

Accompanying letter from Tatham to FPP explains Morris' connection to Edward Morgan Lewis.

1966. February 7. Hobart Morris to David Tatham. als.

Given to FPP by Hobart Morris. Copy of *Edward Morgan Lewis and Robert Frost, 1916-1936*. This paper by Mr. Morris contains copies of a number of letters from the Frosts to the Lewises. Accompanying letter from Morris.

 McGinley, Phyllis

1962. January 23. McGinley to Frost. Larchmont NY. photocopy. Accompanying letter from Martin Bush.

Pierce and Scopes, Albany NY

1933. December 4. Frost to Pierce and Scopes. Order for Marshall's *Life of Washington*. holograph. [Note by FPP: acquired in 1955 with *Selected Poems* first edition from Lockrow's in Albany.]

Piskor, Frank

1961. July 11. Frost to FPP. Ripton VT. tls. [Note by FPP: relates to inscription in *North of Boston*, PS3511.R94 N6 1914.]

Homer Noble Farm
Ripton
Vermont.

July 11, 1961.

Dear Frank:

The colleges and universities can do things like that for poetry when they are presided over by the likes of you. You snatched Phillip Booth I will not say from the burning but from the withering up. Now let him burn. It is up to him to burn. The set-up for him was something to hear. We have done our part. The only thing left to do is to keep him from the fear that we expect too much from him immediately. What a pleasant life stretches ahead of him. The institution belongs of course to the old guard and the great names of the past but I do want it to think with kind condescension when it can find time for the young adventurers in our future.

Thank you from the heart for being what you are.

Ever yours
Robert

Ed Richards

[1935. July 9] Frost to Richards. [South Shaftsbury VT]. photocopy.

Mr. Savage

1949. February 9. Frost to Savage. South Miami FL. photocopy.

Howard Schmitt

1955. June 17. Frost to Schmitt. Ripton VT. photocopy.

Charles Wharton Stork

1921. March 4. Frost to Stork. South Shaftsbury VT. als.
1925. January 24. Frost to Stork. Amherst MA. original telegram.
1932. April 4. Frost to Stork. Amherst MA. als.

A. M. Sullivan

1941. February 10. Frost to Sullivan. Coconut Grove FL. photocopy.
1943. March 4. Sullivan to Frost photocopy.

Miss Winslow

[n.d.] Frost to Winslow. photocopy. Accompanying letter from Howard Applegate.

B. Non-book printed material

1. Magazine and newspaper articles and poems

[Arranged chronologically]

"In the Home Stretch," *Century Magazine*, vol. 92, July, 1916. pp. 383-391. Illustrated by John Wolcott Adams. First printing.

"A Way Out," *The Seven Arts*, vol. 1, February 1917. pp. 347-362. [Note by FPP: first printing.]

"A Group of Poems," *Harpers Magazine*, no. 842, July 1920. pp. 196-199.

"Nothing Gold Can Stay." Typescript of two different versions, one dated July 8, 1922 and one dated March 12, 1924.

"Paul's Wife," [poem] *The London Mercury*, vol. 6, July 1922. pp. 236-239. [Note by FPP: first printing.]

"Stopping by Woods on a Snowy Evening," [poem] *The Chapbook*, no. 36, April 1923. p. 3.

[106] "Robert Frost on Sixtieth Birthday Talks of Joys of Living, Says He'd Like to be Older," *The Amherst Student*, [1934] typed transcript of letter. Accompanying note from Horace Hewlett.

"The Lost Follower," [poem] *Boston Herald, Harvard Tercentenary Issue*, September 13, 1936. p. 8.

[letter to LFB about atomic energy, circa 1945] in Asimov, Isaac. "Tomorrow's Energy," *The American Way*, vol. 8, February 1975. p. 13.

"From Plane to Plane," [poem] *What's New*, no. 130, December 1948. pp. 10-11.

"And All We Call American," pp.28-29 and

"Poetry and School," pp. 30-31, *The Atlantic* , vol. 187. June, 1951. Issue also contains "Robert Frost's America" by Mark Van Doren.

"How Hard It Is to Keep from Being King When It's in You and the Situation," *Proceedings of the American Academy of Arts and Letters and the National Institute of Arts and Letters*, no. 1, second series, 1951. photocopy.

"How Hard It Is Not to Be King When It's In You and In the Situation," [poem] *New York Herald Tribune Book Review*, July 1, 1951. pp. 2-3.

"A Cabin in the Clearing," *Perspectives USA*, no. 4, Summer 1953. pp. 24-25.

"One More Brevity," [poem] *The Atlantic*, vol. 193, June 1954. p. 34.

"Kitty Hawk," [poem] *The Atlantic*, vol. 200, November 1957. pp. 52-56.

"Robert Frost's New Hampshire," *New Hampshire Profiles*, vol. 8, May 1959. pp. 12-19.

"Late Frost: Witty, Wise & Young," *Time*, vol. 76, July 4, 1960. p. 81. Page of various Frost quotes.

"Old Poet in New Land," *Coronet*, vol. 50, September 1961. pp. 97-111. Frost's reflections on Israel. Also reference to Frost on p. 4.

"Sand Dunes," [poem] in Sinclair Oil Corporation. *Plea for a Green Legacy*, ca. 1961.

"Between Prose and Verse," *The Atlantic*, vol. 209. January, 1962. pp. 51-54.

"Seven Poems by Robert Frost," *Life*, vol. 52, March 30, 1962. pp. 60-69. Illustrations by Harvey Schmidt. [Note by FPP: one of the few times Frost is illustrated by a modern painter. Others, most of them, are on the Christmas cards.]

"Nothing More Gentle Than Strength," *New Republic*, vol. 146, April 9, 1962. pp. 21-22.

"Dvoe brodiag v rasputitsu" [Two Tramps in Mud Time], "Dvoe vidiat dvukh" [Two Look at Two], "Zvezdokol" [The Star-Splitter], *Novyi mir [New World]*, vol. 38, no. 8, August 1962. pp. 167-171.

"Witness to Spring," *Topics*, vol. 56, April-May 1963. pp. 7-10.

"To Prayer I Go: the Letters of Robert Frost to Louis Untermeyer," *Saturday Evening Post*, September 14, 1963. pp. 47-59. Introduction by Roger Kahn.

"Consultant's Choice," *The Quarterly Journal* of the Library of Congress, vol. 27, April 1970. pp. 129-169. [Frost poems on pp. 154-155.] [Note by FPP: also an important MacLeish item—poem previously unpublished.]

"Robert Frost's New Hampshire," *New Hampshire Profiles*, vol. 20, April 1971. pp. 74-78.

"Why Wait for Science," [poem] in Kistiakowsky, George. "American Science at the Crossroads," *C&EN*, April 24, 1972. p. 31.

"A Nature Note on Whippoorwills," [poem] *The Coolidge Hill Gazette*, December [n.d.], p. 3. First printing.

2. Chapters from books

Books We Like, Sixty-two Answers, [Boston]: Massachusetts Library Association, 1936. photocopy of Frost's statement pp. 141-142.

3. Interviews

[Arranged chronologically]

Wilmore, Carl. "Finds Famous American Poet in White Mountain Village," *Boston Post*, February 14, 1916. p. 16. negative copy of newspaper page.

Sherrill, John, "An Interview with Robert Frost: A Strange Kind of Laziness," *Guideposts*, vol. 10, August 1955. pp. 1-5.

"Robert Frost Meets the Press," *The Tuftonian*, vol. 13, Winter, 1957. pp. 41-43. transcript of Frost's "Meet the Press" interview on December 23, 1956. Issue also contains:

"Robert Frost" by Deirdre Giles, pp. 5-8.

"What Counts?" *Insert: an Active Anthology for the Creative*, vol. 1, 1962. pp. [5-10]. From Frost's "Meet the Press" interview on December 23, 1956.

"It Takes a Hero to Make a Poem," *Claremont Quarterly*, vol. 5, Spring 1958. pp. 27-34. From a BBC broadcast with C. Day Lewis on September 13, 1957.

Harris, Arthur S. Jr. "A Visit with Robert Frost," *Think*, vol. 24, March 1958. pp. 7-9.

Ciardi, John. "Master Conversationalist at Work," *Saturday Review*, vol. 42, March 21, 1959. pp. 17+. Also in this issue:

"A Native to the Grain of the American Idiom," by Lawrance Thompson, p. 21.

"The Great Event Is Science. The Great Misgiving, the Fear of God, Is That the Meaning of It Shall be Lost," by Robert Frost, p. 18.

Morrison, Chester. "A Visit With Robert Frost, *Look*, vol. 23, March 31, 1959. pp. 76-81.

"Great Libraries Interest Frost," *Syracuse Herald-American*, April 3, 1960. p. 9.

Poirier, Richard. "The Art of Poetry II: Robert Frost," *The Paris Review*, vol. 24., Summer-Fall 1960. pp. 88-120.

Kahn, Roger. "A Visit with Robert Frost," *Saturday Evening Post*, vol. 233, November 19, 1960. pp. 26-30.

Hudson, Arthur Palmer. transcription of tape-recorded conversation with Frost about a trip he made to Kitty Hawk on 1894. March 3, 1961.

Morris, Leavitt. "Supper with Robert Frost," *Christian Science Monitor*, April 6, 1961.

Brooks, Cleanth and Robert Penn Warren with Robert Frost et al. "Conversations on the Craft of Poetry." transcription of the tape recording made to accompany *Understanding Poetry*, NY: Holt, Rinehart and Winston, 1961. pp. 3-18.

4. Addresses

a. In Frost's words

[Arranged chronologically]

"A Monument to After-Thought Unveiled," [high school valedictory address], *Lawrence High School Bulletin*, June, 1892. p. 10.

[Remarks at the dedication of the Wilfred Davison Memorial Library at Bread Loaf, July 21, 1930]. photocopy. Accompanying letter and other material from Dr. Grace Davis.

[Remarks at the memorial service for Edward Morgan Lewis at the University of New Hampshire], May 26, 1936. printed booklet containing all the tributes.

"What Became of New England," [Oberlin commencement address], June 8, 1937. reprinted from *The Oberlin Alumni Magazine*, May 1938.

"Two Lectures by Robert Frost," *Biblia*, vol. 9, February 1938. Contains the texts of two Frost lectures: "Poverty and Poetry"—Haverford College, October 25, 1937, and "The Poet's Next of Kin in a College,"—Princeton University, October 26, 1937.

"Speaking of Loyalty," [remarks at Amherst alumni luncheon, June 19, 1948.] *Amherst Graduates' Quarterly*, No. 148, August 1948. pp. 271-276.

"A Tribute to Wordsworth," [remarks at the celebration at Cornell of the centennial of the death of William Wordsworth, April 20, 1950]. *The Cornell Daily Sun*, vol. 79, March 1, 1963. Supplement.

[Dartmouth commencement address]. *Dartmouth Alumni Magazine*, vol. 47, July 1955. pp. 14-16. Also describes awarding of honorary degree to Frost, pp. 10-11.

[Reading at the American Academy of Arts and Letters] December 11, 1955. *Proceedings* of the American Academy of Arts and Letters, No. 6, 1956. pp. 67-70. Introduction by Glenway Wescott.

"A Talk for Students," [Sarah Lawrence commencement speech], June 7, 1956. booklet distributed by the Fund for the Republic.

"The Future of Man," Proceedings of [panel?] sponsored by Jos. E. Seagram & Sons, Inc. September 29, 1959. photocopy of Frost's statement from pp. 15-17.

[Remarks at the twenty-fifth anniversary dinner of the Academy of American Poets], November 4, 1959. program , pp. 13-16. Accompanying correspondence with Elizabeth Kay.

"Providing for a National Academy of Culture," Hearings before the Senate Committee on Labor and Public Welfare on S. 2207. May 5, 1960. Frost's testimony pp. 9-19.

"'I Want Poets Declared Equal to—'," *New York Times Magazine*, May 15, 1960. pp. 23+.

"Remarks on the Occasion of the Tagore Centenary," *Poetry*, vol. 90, November 1961, pp. 106-119. original and photocopy.

[Excerpts from Frost's Mona Bronfman Sheckman lecture at Sarah Lawrence], April 17, 1962. pamphlet entitled *The Mona Bronfman Sheckman Lectures*. Accompanying correspondence.

[Remarks at the dedication of the Andrew Mellon Library Wing at Choate School]. *The Choate Alumni Bulletin*, vol. 24, Summer 1962. Accompanying letters from Cynthia Walsh and Pauline Anderson. [Note by Dr. Piskor on original folder: Cynthia Walsh was one of my great supporters]

"Robert Frost: Farmer-Teacher," [remarks at the dedication of the Andrews Library at Wooster]. *Wooster Alumni Bulletin*, vol. 76, June 1962. p. 12. Accompanied by newspaper clipping.

"Playing for Mortal Stakes" [remarks at the National Committee of the Amherst Capital Program on the occasion of the announcement of the gift of the Robert Frost Library], September 28, 1962. *Amherst Alumni News*, vol. 15, Fall 1962. pp. 4-10.

[Remarks at 125th anniversary of Mt. Holyoke]. *Mount Holyoke Alumnae Quarterly*, vol. 46, Fall 1962. p. 119.

[Remarks at 50th anniversary of *Poetry Magazine*]. Newspaper clipping [October 1962].

"Playful Talk by Robert Frost of the Academy," [speech at a meeting of the National Institute of Arts and Letters], *Proceedings* of the American Academy of Arts and Letters, second series no. 12, 1962. pp. 180-189.

"Robert Frost on 'Extravagance,'" *Dartmouth Alumni Magazine*, vol. 55, March 1963. pp. 21-24. Frost's last public lecture.

[Remarks at the dedication of the Gordon Keith Chalmers Library at Kenyon College]. *Kenyon Alumni Bulletin*, vol. 21, January-March, 1963. pp. 6-9.

b. Notes by others on Frost addresses

[Arranged alphabetically by reporter]

Calder, Helen. [Note by FPP: My wife Anne's aunt.]

[notes from alumni memorial lecture at University of Massachusetts], October 25, 1961.

[notes from dedication of the Robert Frost library at Amherst], September 29, 1962.

[notes from television interview of Frost], October 23, 1963.

Massachusetts Collegian. [report on Frost's address on October 18, 1934.] typed synopsis.

Staples, Arthur. [report on Frost's lecture, "Vocal Imagination," at Bowdoin College. Reprinted by the college from the *Lewiston Journal*.] photocopy. Accompanying letter from Kenneth Boyer.

5. Broadsides and pamphlets

"Birches." first printing. Bread Loaf Folder, No. 3. Accompanying note from Corinne Davids.

"From Robert Frost," in *Dorothy Canfield Fisher: In Memoriam*. NY: Book-of-the-Month Club, 1958.

"The Poetry of Amy Lowell." n.d. photographic copy of a broadside.

"To a Young Wretch," facsimile of holograph copy used as a Christmas card by the Clifton Waller Barrett Library.

Photofacsimile of Robert Frost poem. Signed "To the Library of St. Lawrence University from Lesley Frost, 1971."

"Something Like a Star." copy of poem hand-lettered by Elizabeth Mount used as a Christmas card by Bob and Betsey Northrup in 1977.

6. Quotes and short anecdotes

7. Books containing Frost poems

New Poems for the Grades. Selected and arranged by a committee of the Sisters of St. Joseph. New York: W. H. Sadlier, 1968. Contains "Design," p. 9 and "The Runaway," p. 54-55.

Robert Frost 1981 Engagement Calendar. New York: Holt, Rinehart and Winston, 1980. Contains poems by Frost and photographs by Dewitt Jones.

II. Material about Frost

A. Biographical

1. Correspondence about Frost

[Arranged alphabetically by correspondent]

Adams, Sherman to David Tatham. March 29, 1966. Lincoln, NH. tls. photocopy.

Booth, Philip to FPP. February 3, 1966. Syracuse, NY. tls. Contains a copy of the review discussed.

Brown, Stuart Gerry to FPP. October 1, 1964. Honolulu, HI. tls. Accompanying correspondence.

Cushman, Robert to R. E. Delmage. "Six Hours with Robert Frost." [describes picking up the Frosts in Utica and driving them to Canton, where Frost was to receive an honorary degree] Accompanying letters to FPP.

[David], Corinne to FPP. Contains an *Old Farmer's Almanac* which Lawrance Thompson feels was the inspiration for "Mending Wall."

Graves, Robert to Gentlemen of the Swedish Academy. February 1963. Spain. als. [draft of letter proposing Frost for Nobel Prize. Never sent because of Frost's death. See illustration on page 110.]

Hall, Donald to FPP. October 6, 1992. Danbury, NH. tls.

Johnson, A. E. two diary entries about Frost dated March 3, 1932 and July 31, 1955.

Lee, W. Storrs to FPP. December 24, 1991. Kihei, HI. tls.

Meredith, William to FPP. November 2, 1970. Pittsburgh, PA. tls. [Note by FPP: this letter was in response to a critical letter on Frost in one of the magazines, probably the *Saturday Review*.]

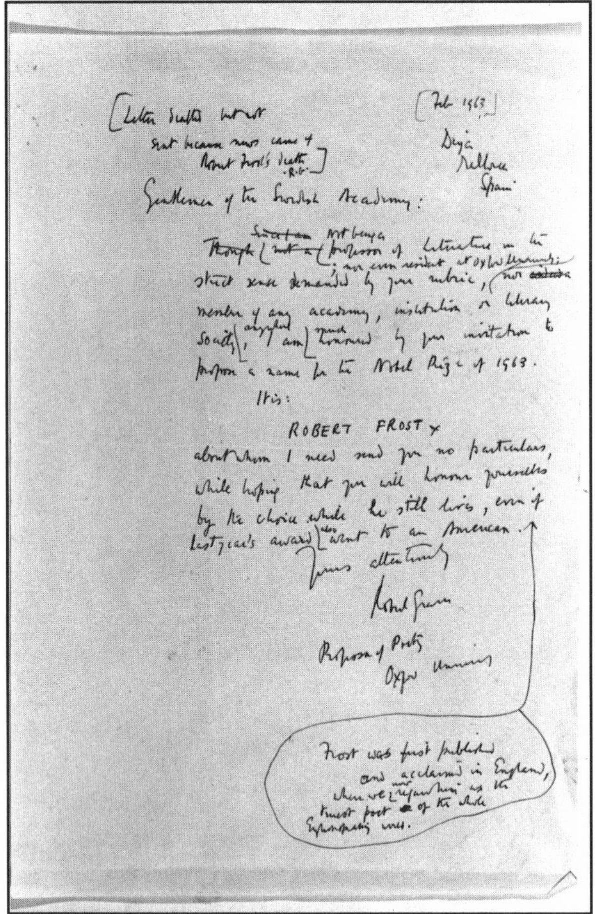

[Letter drafted but not sent because news came of Robert Frost's death. R.G.]

[Feb 1963]

Deyá
Mallorca
Spain

Gentlemen of the Swedish Academy:

Though not being a professor of Literature in the strict sense demanded by your rubric, nor member of any academy, institution or literary society, I am much honoured by your invitation to propose a name for the Nobel Prize of 1963.

It is:

ROBERT FROST

about whom I need send you no particulars, while hoping that you will honour yourselves by the choice while he still lives, even if last year's award also went to an American.

Yours attentively

Robert Graves

Professor of Poetry
Oxford University

Frost was first published and acclaimed in England, where we now regard him as the finest poet of the whole English-speaking world.

Draft of a letter from Robert Graves to the Swedish Academy proposing Frost for a Nobel Prize. Frost's death intervened and the letter was never sent.

Powell, Wesley to David Tatham. April 20, 1966. Hampton Falls, NH. photocopy of tls. [Note from Tatham to FPP: Wesley Powell was governor of New Hampshire in the late '50s and early '60s.]

Rand, Frank Prentice to David Tatham. April 19, 1966. Maitland FL. photocopy of tls.

Reinecke, Warren to FPP. February 27, 1992. Grinnell, IA. tls.

Tatham, David to FPP. July 15, 1963. Syracuse University. tls.

Tatham, David to Bruce Catton. August 12, 1964. copy signed.

Thompson, Lawrance to David Tatham. September 3, 1970. Princeton, NJ. photocopy of tls.

Van Egmond, Peter to FPP. February 20, 1992. Silver Springs, MD. tls.

a. Individual articles

[Arranged alphabetically by author]

Atkinson, Brooks. "Letters of Robert Frost Reveal the Poet as a Determined, Self-Centered Man, *New York Times*, September 11, 1964.

Basler, Roy. "Lobbyist for the Arts," *Quarterly Journal* of the Library of Congress, April 1974.

Baxter, Sylvester. "New England's New Poet," *The American Review of Reviews*, vol. 51, April 1915. pp. 432+.

Cane, Melville. "Robert Frost: an Intermittent Intimacy," *The American Scholar*, vol. 40, Winter 1970-71. pp. 158-166.

Ciardi, John. "Robert Frost: Two Anecdotes," *Saturday Review*, vol. 4, September 3, 1977. p. 48.

Cobb, Stanwood. "How Success Came to Robert Frost," unpublished paper. Accompanying letter by Martin Bush. [Note by FPP: Stanwood Cobb was the headmaster of the school Lesley Frost Ballantine's daughters attended.]

Cook, Reginald. "A Walk with Robert Frost," *Yankee*, November 1955. pp. 19-26.

Davison, Peter. "'I Want People to Understand Me. But I Want Them to Understand Me Wrong," *New England Monthly*, vol. 2, June 1985. pp. 42-44.

Dendinger, Lloyd. "Robert Frost in Birmingham," *Ball State University Forum*, pp. 47-52.

Dickey, James. "Robert Frost, Man and Myth," *The Atlantic*, vol. 218, November 1966. pp. 53-56.

Dole, Jeremy. "The Frost-Hoblin Papers," *Country Journal*, December 1976. p. 41-43. [Note by FPP: the letters are not in Frost's handwriting (or maybe it was in 1905?). They may have been copied or written by his wife for him.]

Drury, Michael. "Robert Frost," *McCall's*, vol. 87, April 1960, pp. 80+.

Drury, Michael. "Robert Frost: His Power and His Glory," *Reader's Digest*, vol. 78, April 1961. pp. 270-276. Condensation of above article in *McCall's*.

Francis, Robert. "Face to Face," *Intellectual Digest*, vol. 3, May 1973. pp. 49-56. [from the book *Frost: a Time to Talk*.]

Francis, Robert. "Frost as Apple-Peeler," *New England Review*, vol. 1, Autumn, 1978. pp. 32-39. Accompanying note to FPP from M. Robin Barone. Also contains "Fall," a poem by Philip Booth. p. 82.

Garner, Dwight. "Acquainted with the Night," *The Boston Globe Magazine*, January 24, 1993. pp. 14-21.

Gentry, Chisholm, "The Resurrection of Robert Frost," *Vermont Magazine*, vol. 1, November-December 1989. pp. 36+.

Grade, Arnold. "Robert Frost: Every Poem He Wrote is a Kind of Hide and Seek," Rochester *Democrat and Chronicle*, March 24, 1974. p. 6H.

"The Grand Old Man of Poetry," *The Sunday Star Magazine*, June 26, 1960. pp. 18-22.

Haines, John. "Robert Frost," *Now and Then*, No. 77, Autumn 1948. pp. 9-11.

Harris, Mark. "The Pride and Wisdom of Two Great Old Poets, Sandburg...Frost: A Novelist's Illuminating Visit," *Life*, vol. 51, December 1, 1961. pp. 104-122. [Note by FPP: important essay.]

Holt, Rinehart, and Winston. *Annual Report*, 1962. pp.2-3, 8.

Lathem, Edward. "Robert Frost: Assailant," *The New England Galaxy*, vol. 6, Spring 1965. pp. 27-29.

Lowell, Robert. "Robert Frost: 1875-1963," *New York Review of Books*, Special Issue, 1963, p. 7.

McGlynn, Frank E. "The New Hampshire Aspect of Robert Frost," *News and Notes* of the Vermont Historical Society, vol. 14, June 1963. pp. 73-76.

McLam, James, "My Business with a Poet," *Vermont Life*, vol. 18, Autumn 1963. pp. 41-43.

"'Mending Wall' in Moscow," *The New York Times Magazine*, September 16, 1962. p. 34.

Meryman, Richard. "Sherman Adams: the Quintessential Doer," *Yankee*, vol. 42, April 1978. pp. 70-71. [Frost discussed on p. 71.]

Monteiro, George, "The Brazilian Academy's Tribute to Frost, *The South Carolina Review*, vol. 21, Fall 1988. pp. 3-4.

Morse, Stearns. "The Wholeness of Robert Frost," *The Virginia Quarterly Review*, vol. 19, Summer 1943. pp. 412-416.

Nash, Ray. "The Poet and the Pirate," *The New Colophon*, vol. 2, February 1950. pp. 311-321.

Nethercot, Arthur. "Robert Frost," *College Verse*, vol. 8, December 1938. p. 26. Also contains:

"The Robert Frost Poetry Library," pp. 26+.

"Revelation" [poem] by Frost, p. 27.

Nordell, Roderick. "A Look at Two Baseball-loving Poets, *Christian Science Monitor*, May 26, 1976. p. 23.

"Of G. Gold, and P. Corn, and R. Frost," *The Monthly Letter of the Limited Editions Club*, No. 216, July 1950. pp. 1-4.

"On the Side," *Island Advantages*, vol. 29, January 30, 1964. p. 1. [reports on a letter from Daniel Smythe in which he quotes a story told by Frost.] Accompanying letter from Marjorie Smith.

"Pawky Poet," *Time*, vol. 56, October 9, 1950. pp. 76-82.

"A Poet's Pilgrimage," *Life*, vol. 43, September 23, 1957. pp. 109-112.

Quinan, Dorothy Cheney. "Poet is a Praise Word," *Yankee*, September 1969. pp. 90+.

Reeve, F. D. "Robert Frost Confronts Khrushchev," *The Atlantic*, vol. 212, September 1963. pp. 33-39.

Reston, James. "A Personal Communique from Robert Frost," *New York Times*, October 27, 1957. [Note by FPP: an important item.]

Richards, Norman. "Robert Frost's New England," *United Mainliner*, December 1968, vol. 12.

Samuel, Rinna. "Robert Frost in Israel," *New York Times Book Review*, April 23, 1961. pp. 42-43.

"Season's Greetings from Robert Frost," *The Chronicle of Higher Education*, vol. 39, December 16, 1992. p. B64.

Sergeant, Elizabeth. "England Discovers Robert Frost," *The Atlantic*, vol. 205, May 1960. pp. 61-65. [Note by FPP: an important short essay on the English years.]

Sheehy, Donald. "(Re)Figuring Love: Robert Frost in Crisis, 1938-1942," *The New England Quarterly*, vol. 63, June 1990, pp. 179-231.

Smythe, Daniel. "But What Does a Poet-in-Residence Do?" *Phi Kappa Phi Journal*, vol. 50, Spring 1970. pp. 25-27.

Smythe, Daniel. "A Visit with Robert Frost," manuscript dated May 1939.

Speirs, Russell. "Lost with Frost," *Yankee*, vol. 35, January 1971. pp. 80-83.

Stetson, Fred. "The Gully Years: with Robert Frost in South Shaftsbury," *Vermont Life*, vol. 47, Winter 1992. pp. 18-23.

Swain, Raymond. "To Know Greatness," *New Hampshire Profiles*, vol. 15, February 1966. pp. 20+.

Tatham, David. "Robert Frost's Franconia Mountains, *Appalachia*, vol. 30, December 1964. pp. 248-249. Library's copy inscribed by author to FPP. Accompanying letter by Tatham to FPP.

Thompson, Lawrance. "The California Boyhood of Robert Frost," *Princeton Alumni Weekly*, vol. 57, November 9, 1956. pp. 13-15.

Thompson, Lawrance. "The California Boyhood of Robert Frost," *University*, no. 2, Fall 1959. pp. 16-20.

Thompson, Lawrance. "Frost: a Warning on Life," *Boston Globe*, September 25, 1966.

Thompson, Lawrance. "Robert Frost's Affection for New Hampshire," *Historical New Hampshire*, vol. 22, Summer 1967. pp. 3-26. [Note by FPP: an important Thompson article.]

Trohan, Walter. "JFK Snubbed Robert Frost," *Human Events*, vol. 21, April 6, 1963. p. 13.

Udall, Stewart L. "'...and Miles to Go Before I Sleep': Robert Frost's Last Adventure," *New York Times Magazine*, June 11, 1972. pp. 18+. [Note by FPP: a useful essay by a close friend]

Van Dore, Edrie. "October, Spelled with Bittersweet and Rare Blue Gentians," *Christian Science Monitor*, October 12, 1962.

Van Dore, Wade. "North of Robert Frost," *Christian Science Monitor*, May 2, 1962.

Van Dore, Wade. "Piers Plowman and Robert Frost," *Christian Science Monitor*, July 26, 1970.

"The Visitor," *Time*, vol. 69, June 24, 1957. p. 62.

Walen, Harry. "A Man Named Robert Frost," *The English Journal*, October 1966. pp. 860-862.

"The Young Frost: A Yank from Yankville," *The Times Literary Supplement*, No. 3433, December 14, 1967. p. 1201+.

b. Folders of newspaper clippings and fliers

Frost's trip to Israel
Frost's trip to the Soviet Union
Frost and the Kennedy inauguration
Reports on public lectures and readings
[Note by FPP on Poetry Center Program for 1961-62: Robert Frost appeared April 12, 1963 (a regular stop-over on his way South).]
Miscellaneous clippings about Frost

3. Frost's professional activities as a poet

Memberships
Activities in 1955 designed to save *Poetry Magazine* [Note by FPP: Robert Frost participated as a manuscript contributor and performer.]

4. Honors

a. Honorary degree citations

University of Cincinnati (1954)
University of Cambridge (1957)
University of Detroit (1960)
University of Michigan (1962)

b. Literary prizes

Gold Medal of the National Institute of Arts and Letters for Poetry (1939)
Huntington Hartford Foundation (1958)
Gold Medal for Distinguished Service of the Poetry Society of America (1958)
MacDowell Medal (1962). Accompanying letter by Gwen Haste describes the award ceremony.
Bollingen Poetry Prize (1963)

c. Poet Laureate of Vermont

d. A Centennial Tribute to Robert Frost, March 23, 1974.

e. Robert Frost Day, March 26, 1974

Proclamation of Robert Frost Day by Governor of New Hampshire. Signed copy with seal.
  Small copies of text. 1 signed.
Frost Commemorative Stamp
  First day covers, blocks of stamps, etc.
  Philatelic information about the stamp

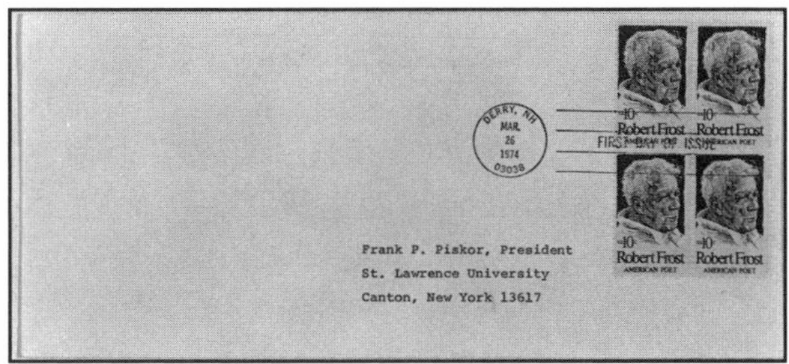

First day cover of stamp issued March 26, 1974 to celebrate the centennial of Frost's birth. The design is a pencil drawing by Paul Calle.

  First Day of Issue Ceremony
    Programs and memorabilia
    Typed copies of remarks by Mrs. Arthur Burns and Dr. Piskor
    Smythe, Daniel. "Robert Frost Centenary Celebrations," Poetry Society of N.H. *Newsletter*, February-March, 1975. pp. 1-7. signed by author. Accompanying letters by Smythe.

Press releases and newspaper clippings, including reprint of Piskor talk in the *Bulletin* of the Friends of ODY Library.
Correspondence by Dr. Piskor concerning the program

f. Senate Resolution on Frost's 75th birthday.

5. Frost and education

a. Frost's opinions on education
[Arranged chronologically]

"How a Poet Teaches," *The New Student*, vol. 5, January 6, 1926. pp. 1+.
Frost, Robert. "The Manumitted Student," *The New Student*, vol. 6, January 12, 1927. pp. 5-7.
Newdick, Robert. "Robert Frost and the American College," *The Journal of Higher Education*, vol. 7, May 1936. pp. 237-243.
Newdick, Robert. "Robert Frost, Teacher and Educator," *Journal of Higher Education*, vol. 7, June 1936. pp. 342-344. [Note by Dr. Piskor: An important bibliography.]
"Poet Would Give Young Folks More Time to Find Themselves," *Free Press and Times* [Burlington VT] August 19, 1936. typed transcription. Accompanying correspondence.
Larson, Mildred. "'No False Curves': Robert Frost on Education," *School and Society*, vol. 72, September 16, 1950. pp. 1-189.
Cook, Reginald. "Notes on Frost the Lecturer," *The Quarterly Journal of Speech*, [n.d., circa 1953-55] pp. 127-132.
"Robert Frost: Opinions on Education, Thought," *The Amherst Student*, vol. 83, October 19, 1953.
Bowie, Carole. "Poet Frost Would Like High Schools 'Toned Up'," *Washington Post*, May 10, 1962.

b. Frost and Syracuse University

Items relating to Frost's 1932 visit
Items relating to Frost's 1959 visit

c. Frost and Middlebury College

General Middlebury-related items
Bread Loaf items

d. Frost and Amherst College

General Amherst-related items
Items relating to Frost's teaching at Amherst
Items relating to Frost Library
Special Robert Frost issue of *Touchstone*, vol. 4, February 1939.
Items relating to Frost and the town of Amherst MA

e. Frost and Dartmouth College

Items relating to Frost as a student
Items relating to Frost's teaching at Dartmouth
Items relating to honors received from Dartmouth as an adult
General Dartmouth-related items

f. Frost and other educational institutions

Agnes Scott College
Bennington
Colgate
Duke
Exeter
Franconia College
Goucher
Grinnell
Hebrew University
Mark Hopkins College
Robert Frost School
Robert Lee Frost Elementary School
Trinity
- Special Frost edition of *Trinity Tripod* signed by Frost. [Note by FPP: Bacon Collamore to whom Frost refers in his inscription was a Hartford CT businessman and a Frost-Robinson collector.]
- Other Trinity-related material

University of Massachusetts
University of Michigan
Wesleyan
Windham College

6. Tributes to Frost after his death

Calder, Helen B. to FPP. als. [letter about Frost's death]
Obituaries
Memorial Services
  Amherst
    Special Frost Issue of *The Amherst Student*, February 18, 1963. [Note by Dr. Piskor: One of the letters is by Richard Wilbur, recent Library of Congress Poet Laureate.]
  Harvard
  Middlebury
Tributes in print
Joint Resolution R-33 expressing appreciation to Frost—*Congressional Record*, January 29, 1963. pp. 1211-1212.
Robert Frost Memorial Drive
Robert Frost Plaza
Information on Frost's grave
Miscellaneous tributes in non-print form

B. Material about Frost's poems

1. Articles about Frost's poems in general

[Arranged alphabetically by author]

Adams, J. Donald. "Speaking of Books," *New York Times Book Review*, November 11, 1959.

Adams, J. Donald. "Speaking of Books," *New York Times Book Review*, March 22, 1959. p. 2. Also contains: "Auden on Frost" and "Frost—His Universality" and three poems by Frost.

Anderson, Charles. "Robert Frost, 1874-1963," *Saturday Review*, vol. 46, February 23, 1963. pp. 17-20. Also contains:
"Robert Frost: Teacher-at-Large" by John S. Dickey. pp. 21+,
"The Classicism of Robert Frost" by John Frederick Nims,

"Robert Frost: to Earthward" by John Ciardi. p. 24
[Note by FPP: an important issue.]

Baker, Carlos. "Frost on the Pumpkin," *The Georgia Review*, vol. 11, Summer 1957. pp. 117-131. Also contains an editorial reference on p. 116. [Note by FPP: an insightful analysis by this famous Princeton professor.]

Ball State University Forum. vol. 11, Winter 1970. entire issue devoted to Frost. Article by LFB signed in one of the library's copies. [Note by FPP: important and rare.]

Beach, Joseph. "Robert Frost," *The Yale Review*, vol. 43, Winter 1954. pp. 204-217. [Note by FPP: the comparative comments in relation to Emerson on pp. 210-211 are particularly interesting.]

Bennett, Paul. "Robert Frost: 'Best-Printed' U.S. Author, and His Printer, Spiral Press," *Publishers' Weekly*, vol. 185, March 2, 1964. pp. 82-90.

Bracker, Milton. "The 'Quietly Overwhelming' Robert Frost," *The New York Times Magazine*, November 30, 1958. pp. 15+.

Cady, Edwin. "Robert Frost as a Modern Poet," *Syracuse Daily Orange*, April 21, 1959.

Cary, Michael. "'Going Home from Company Means Coming to Our Senses': the Theme of Departure in the Poetry of Robert Frost." typescript. [Note by FPP: Carey was an independent study student at SLU who used my collection.]

Cestre, Charles. "Amy Lowell, Robert Frost and Edwin Arlington Robinson," *The Johns Hopkins Alumni Magazine*, vol. 14, March 1926. pp. 363-388.

Ciardi, John. "Robert Frost: American Bard, *Saturday Review*, vol. 45, March 24, 1962. pp. 15-17+. [Note by FPP: Ciardi closes with the growing concern of the literary community that Frost is not being recognized by the Swedish Academy for the Nobel Prize. See Graves letter, p. 109.]

Cook, Reginald. "Frost on Frost: the Making of Poems," *American Literature*, vol. 28, March 1956. pp. 62-72.

Cowley, Malcolm. "Frost: A Dissenting Opinion," *The New Republic*, vol. 3, September 11, 1944. pp. 312-313. [Note by FPP: an important dissent.]

Cowley, Malcolm. "The Case Against Mr. Frost: II," *The New Republic*, vol. 3, September 18, 1944. pp. 345-347.

Cox, Sidney. "Robert Frost and Poetic Fashion," *American Scholar*, vol. 18, Winter 1948-49. pp. 78-86.

Cox, Sidney. "The Courage to Be New," *Vermont History*, vol. 22, 1954. pp. 119-126.

Foster, Charles Howell. "Robert Frost and the New England Tradition," *University of Colorado Studies*, vol. 2, October 1945. pp. 370-381. Accompanying letter from Foster to "Stuart." [Note by FPP: an important essay.]

Fowle, Rosemary. "The Indwelling Spider: An Aspect of the Poetry of Robert Frost," *Papers* of the Michigan Academy of Science, Arts, and Letters, vol. 37, 1951. pp. 437-444.

Francis, Robert, Charles W. Cole, and Reginald L Cook, "On Robert Frost," *The Massachusetts Review*, Winter 1963, pp. 237-249.

Frederick, John T. "The Robust Wisdom of Robert Frost," *The Rotarian*, December 1972. pp. 36-37.

Haines, J. W. "The Dymock Poets," *Gloucestershire Countryside*, 1931-34. pp. 131-133.

Hearn, Thomas K. Jr. "Making Sweetbreads Do: Robert Frost and Moral Empiricism," *The New England Quarterly*, vol. 49, March 1976, pp. 65-81.

Hiers, John. "Robert Frost's Quarrel with Science and Technology," *The Georgia Review*, vol. 25, Summer 1971. pp. 182-205. [Note by FPP: an important analysis—frequently cited.]

Hodgson, Ralph. [remarks on Frost as recorded by John Mayfield in an interview on August 26, 1961.] Accompanying letter and photograph by Mayfield.

Hoeller, Hildegarde, "Evolution and Metaphor in Robert Frost's Poetry," *South Carolina Review*, vol. 22, Fall 1990 pp. 127-135.

Jamieson, Paul F. "Robert Frost: Poet of Mountain Land," *Appalachia*, December 1959. pp. 471-480. One copy signed by author. Accompanying letter from Jamieson to FPP.

Lathem, Edward Connery. "Editing Robert Frost," *Dartmouth Alumni Magazine*, February 1972, p. 24-27.

Lathem, Edward Connery. "Introduction: The Poetry of Robert Frost," Imprint Society, 1971. One of 250 copies. Reprint version of Lathem's introduction to the Imprint Society's issuance of *The Poetry of Robert Frost*. Accompanying letter from Lathem.

Lewis, Claude. "A Poet's Road to Wisdom," *Philadelphia Inquirer*. [Note by FPP: a sensitive, insightful column]

"A Lover's Quarrel with the World," *Time*, February 8, 1963. p. 84.

Lycette, Ronald L. "The Vortx Points of Robert Frost," *Ball State University Forum*, vol. 14, 1973, pp. 54-59.

Lyle, Charles C., Jr. "Goethe and Robert Frost." typescript with accompanying correspondence. [Note by FPP: "Collis" Lyle headed the Modern Languages and Literatures Department at St. Lawrence in my time.]

McCoy, Donald Edward. "Robert Frost: The Reception and Development of His Poetry." Entry from *Dissertation Abstracts International* describing this 1952 University of Illinois dissertation.

MacLeish, Archibald. "Robert Frost and New England," *National Geographic*, vol. 149, April 1976. pp. 438-444. Also contains: "Look of a Land Beloved," pp. 444-468. [Photographic essay by Dewitt Jones, illustrating Frost's poetry.]

Meredith, William. Typescript of introduction of Frost at the Poetry Center of the YM-YWHA, April 10, 1961. Accompanying letter by Meredith. [Note by FPP: Frost read en route to Florida]

Monteiro, George. "The Facts on Frost," *South Carolina Review*, vol. 22, Fall 1989. pp. 87-96.

Montgomery, Marion. "Robert Frost and His Use of Barriers: Man vs. Nature Toward God," *The South Atlantic Quarterly*, vol. 57, Summer 1958. pp. 339-353.

Mulder, William. "Freedom and Form: Robert Frost's Double Discipline," *The South Atlantic Quarterly*, vol. 54, July 1955. pp. 386-393.

The New Hampshire Troubadour, Vol. 16, November 1946. Entire issue devoted to Frost. First printing of "Our Getaway" on p. 9.

O'Donnell, W. G. "Robert Frost and New England: a Reevaluation," *The Yale Review*, vol. 37, Summer 1948. pp. 698-712. [Note by FPP: an important reevaluation—often referred to. Compare with George Monteiro's recent book.]

Ogilvie, John. "From Woods to Stars: A Pattern of Imagery in Robert Frost's Poetry," *The South Atlantic Quarterly*, vol. 58, Winter 1959. pp. 64-76.

O'Meara, Stephen James. "Robert Frost: Poet of the Night," *Sky and Telescope*, June 1992. pp. 692-693.

Oster, Judith. "The Figure a Marriage Makes," *South Carolina Review*, vol. 22, 1989. pp. 109-119.

Parisi, Joseph. "Robert Frost," in *Voices and Visions: Viewer's Guide*. Chicago: American Library Association, 1987. pp. 10-14.

Parsons, Thornton. "Thoreau, Frost, and the American Humanist Tradition," *The Emerson Society Quarterly*, No. 33, Fourth Quarter, 1963. pp. 33-43.

Pearce, Roy Harvey. "The Poet as Person," *The Yale Review*, vol. 41, Spring 1952. pp. 421-440. [Note by FPP: Frost discussed in the context of other poets. Note particularly T. S. Eliot, pp. 427-429]

Pearce, Roy Harvey. "Frost's Momentary Stay," *Kenyon Review*, vol. 23, Spring 1961. pp. 258-273. Reprint copy signed by author.

Perkins, David. "Robert Frost and Romantic Irony," *South Carolina Review*, vol. 22, Fall 1989. pp. 33-37.

Peters, Joan. "Education by Poetry: Robert Frost's Departure from the Modern Critical Tradition," *South Carolina Review*, vol. 21, Fall 1988. pp. 27-37.

Poirier, Richard, "Robert Frost: the Sound of Love and the Love of Sound," *The Atlantic*, vol. 233, April 1974. pp. 50-55.

Ratiner, Steven. "Robert Frost, An American Voice," *Christian Science Monitor*, November 23, 1981. p. 20.

Sanders, David A. "Frost's Divided Narrator: Voice and Drama in 'Home Burial' and 'Out, Out—'," *The South Carolina Review*, vol. 24, Fall 1991. pp. 31-42. Also contains:
"An Ecological Approach to Frost's Poetry" by Michael J. McDowell, pp. 92-100.
"The Other E. Thomas: a Source for Frost's 'Night of Frost'," pp. 153-155.

Sergeant, Elizabeth Shepley. "Robert Frost's Poetry," *New York Herald Tribune Sunday Forum*, January 22, 1961.

Simmons, Tom. "Geography of the Mind," *Christian Science Monitor*, [n.d.]

South Carolina Review, vol. 19, special issue, Summer 1987. entire issue devoted to Frost.

Stafford, William. "The Terror in Robert Frost," *The New York Times Magazine*, August 18, 1974. pp. 24+. [Note by FPP: a controversial essay—important.]

Tatara, Walter T. "Robert Frost: Swinger of Birches," *New Hampshire Profiles*, vol. 16, January 1967. pp. 30-33.

Trilling, Lionel. "A Speech on Robert Frost: A Cultural Episode," *Partisan Review*, vol. 26, Summer 1959. pp. 445-452. With two letters to the editor on the speech—*New York Times Book Review*, May, 24, 1959. p. 42.

Van Doren, Mark. "The Permanence of Robert Frost," *The American Scholar*, vol. 5, Spring 1936. pp. 190-198.

Watts, Harold. "Three Entities and Robert Frost," *Bucknell Review*, vol. 5, December 1955. pp. 19-38.

Wheat, Maxwell C. "Robert Frost and the Edge of the Woods," *Nature Study*, vol. 27, Winter 1973-4. p. 1. Also contains:
"Robert Frost—Poet-Ecologist" by John A. Gustafson, p. 2.
"Robert Frost and Birds" by Maxwell D. Wheat, Jr., pp. 3-5.
"Frost Among the Stars" by Percy M. Proctor, pp. 7-8.
"Douglas E. Wade on Robert Frost," p. 8.

Whicher, George. "Frost at Seventy," *The American Scholar*, vol. 14, Autumn 1945. pp. 405-414. [Note by FPP: an early commentary on Frost and the Transcendentalists written by a close Amherst professorial friend.]

Winters, Yvor. "Robert Frost: or, the Spiritual Drifter as Poet," *The Sewanee Review*, vol. 56, Autumn 1948. pp. 564-596. [Note by FPP: this very critical essay was quite controversial when written—an important contribution.]

[Author unknown] "New England Through the Eyes of Robert Frost." carbon copy of a paper on Frost. Accompanying letter by James Carr.

2. Articles about specific poems

[Arranged alphabetically by poem title]

[After Apple-Picking]

Fleissner, Robert F. "Frost as Ironist: 'After Apple-picking' and the Preautumnal Fall," *South Carolina Review*, vol. 21, Fall 1988. pp. 50-57.

[Auspex]

"Robert Frost: At Heart a Latin Student," *Pompeiiana Newsletter*, vol. 13, January, 1987. p. 3. Accompanying letter from Marian V. D. Stone.

[Come In]

Sperry, Dean. "An Analysis of 'Come In' by Robert Frost." typescript. [Note by FPP: Sperry was an independent study student at SLU who used my collection.]

[Dust of Snow]

"'Dust of snow' by Robert Frost," *The Courier*, No. 27, 1967. p. 16.

[For John F. Kennedy, His Inauguration]

Udall, Stewart L. "Frost's 'Unique Gift Outright'," *The New York Times Magazine*, March 26, 1961. pp. 12+

Küpper, Karl Josef. "Amerikanische Lyrik und Amerikakunde: Die Interpretation von Gedichten mit geschichtlich-gesellschaftlicher Thematik," *Der Fremdsprachliche Unterricht*, vol. 9, May 1975. pp. 24-30. [Frost discussion on pp. 29-30.]

Shapiro, Harvey. "Story of the Poem," *The New York Times Magazine*, January 15, 1961. pp. 6+

[Home Burial]

Katz, Sandra. "'The World is Evil': Personal Experience Dramatized in 'Home Burial'," *South Carolina Review*, vol. 23, Fall 1990. pp. 122-126.

[The Later Minstrel]

Thompson, Lawrance. "An Early Frost Broadside," *The New Colophon*, vol. 1, January 1948. pp. 5-12. Special presentation booklet made for FPP by John Mayfield. Signed by Lawrance Thompson. original and photocopy.

[Not Quite Social]

Broderick, John. "Not Quite Poetry: Analysis of a Robert Frost Manuscript, *Manuscripts*, vol. 20, Spring 1968. pp. 28-31.

[Paul's Wife]

Hoffman, Daniel G. "Robert Frost's Paul Bunyan: A Frontier Hero in New England Exile," *Midwest Folklore*, pp. 13-18.

 [Stopping by Woods]

Ciardi, John. "Robert Frost: The Way to the Poem," *The Saturday Review*, vol.41, April 12, 1958. pp. 13+. With two pages of letters to the editor on the article.

Fisher, Sally. "Robert Frost and the Prime Ministers," *Yankee*, vol. 38, December 1974. pp. 34-39.

McLaughlin, Charles. "Two Views of Poetic Unity," *The University of Kansas City Review*, vol. 22, Summer 1956. pp. 309-316.

Van Dore, Wade. "'I'd Rather believe in Inspiration…'," *Yankee*, vol. 35, November 1971, pp. 116+.

[Subverted Flower]

Weltman, Sharon Aronofsky. "The Least of It: Metaphor, Metamorphosis, and Synecdoche in Frost's 'The Subverted Flower'," *South Carolina Review*, vol.22, Fall 1989. pp. 71-78.

3. Reviews of books by Frost

[Arranged alphabetically by book title]

A Boy's Will

Bieganowski, Ronald. "Robert Frost's *A Boy's Will* and Henri Bergson's *Creative Evolution*,' *South Carolina Review*, vol. 21, Fall 1988. pp. 9-16.

Pound, Ezra. *Poetry*, vol. 2, May, 1913. pp. 72-74. [Note by FPP: important review of *A Boy's Will* by Ezra Pound—the first review.]

A Further Range

Morley, Christopher. "A Further Range," reprint from *Book of the Month Club News*. [n.d.]

In the Clearing

Booth, Philip. "Journey Out of a Dark Forest," *New York Times Book Review*, March 25, 1962. p. 1+.

Church, Richard. "The Riddle of the Universe," *Country Life*, vol. 132, September 27, 1962. pp. 741-723. [Note by FPP: a short, but significant, essay relating Steinbeck, Frost, and Wordsworth as only an Englishman could.]

Gold, Bill. "Robert Frost Awaits World's Verdict," *Washington Post*, March 26, 1962. p. B-18.

Holmes, John. "All the Robert Frosts Are in His New Book, 'In the Clearing'…," *Christian Science Monitor*, March 29, 1962. p. 13.

Kinnaird, Clark. *New York Journal-American*, March 26, 1962. p. 32.

McG., M. "New Frost Anthology Marks Poet's Birthday, *The Sunday Star*, March 25, 1962. p. C-5.

O'Donnell, William G. "Robert Frost at Eighty-eight," *The Massachusetts Review*, vol. 4, Autumn, 1962. pp. 213-218.

"Step and Speech are Lively as Poet Frost Observes a Birthday," *National Observer*, April 1, 1962. p. 3.

Time, vol. 79, March 30, 1962. p. 84.

Wilbur, Richard. "Poems That Soar and Sing and Charm," *New York Herald Tribune—Books Section*, March 25, 1962. p. 3. Also contains "Roger Kahn Writes of His Lively Interest in Robert Frost," p. 3+.

4. Reviews of books about Frost

[Arranged alphabetically by author]

[Anderson, Margaret Bartlett. *Robert Frost and John Bartlett: the Record of a Friendship*]

Reynolds, Horace. "The Sentence is a Sound," *Christian Science Monitor*, December 26, 1963.

[ad for the book with quotes from reviews], *New York Times Book Review*, November 3, 1963. p. 9.

[Brower, Reuben A. *The Poetry of Robert Frost: Constellations of Intention*]

Thompson, Lawrance. "The Verse of the Poet Reread," *The New York Times Book Review*, June 23, 1963. p. 6.

[Clymer, W. B. Shubrick and Charles Green. *Robert Frost: a Bibliography*]

Holmes, John. "Poetry Now," *Boston Herald*, [?] 1937. p. 5. [Note by FPP: Holmes was a Tufts University Poet-in-Residence and a friend of Frost.]

[Cook, Reginald. *The Dimensions of Robert Frost*]

Frankenberg, Lloyd. "New Slants at Old Stars," *New York Times Book Review*, July 6, 1958. p. 4.

Langbaum, Robert. "An Excellent Guide to Frost," *Herald Tribune Book Review*, July 6, 1958, p. 4.

[Cox, Hyde and Edward Connery Lathem. *Selected Prose of Robert Frost*]

Craig, Armour. "Views and Interviews," *New York Times Book Review*, July 24, 1966. pp. 4-5.

[Cox, Sidney. *Robert Frost, the Original 'Ordinary' Man*]

Mayfield, John. "Robert Frost, the Original 'Ordinary' Man," *Fort Worth Star-Telegram and Sunday Record*, April 14, 1929. Accompanying letter by Mayfield.

[Cox, Sidney. *A Swinger of Birches*]

Jarrell, Randall. "In Pursuit of Beauty," *New York Times Book Review*, March 10, 1957.

[Gould, Jean. *Robert Frost: The Aim Was Song*]

Daiches, David. "The Many Faces of a Poet," *New York Times Book Review*, September 20, 1964. p. 5.

[letter to the editor by Gould about David Daiche's review of her book], *New York Times Book Review* October 11, 1964. p. 36.

[Grade, Arnold. *Family Letters of Robert and Elinor Frost*]

Smythe, Daniel. "The Frosts, Robert and Elinor," Peoria IL *Journal-Star*, December 2, 1972. p. C-10.

[Lathem, Edward Connery, editor. *Robert Frost: Farm-Poultryman*]

Engle, Paul. "Pullets and Poetry," *New York Times Book Review*, [n.d.]

[Lathem, Edward Connery. *Interviews with Robert Frost*]

Craig, Armour. with review of Cox and Lathem's *Selected Prose of Robert Frost*.

Hicks, Granville, "Robert Frost Revisited," *Saturday Review*, vol. 49, July 9, 1966. pp. 23-24.

[Lathem, Edward Connery, editor. *The Poetry of Robert Frost*]

Jacobson, Dan. "Verry Amurk'n," *The Review*, no. 25, Spring 1971. pp. 3-10.

[Lathem, Edward Connery. *Selected Prose of Robert Frost*]

Hicks, Granville. with review of Lathem's *Interviews with Robert Frost*.

[*The Letters of Robert Frost to Louis Untermeyer*]

"Ever Yours, Robert," *Time*, September 20, 1963. pp. 102, 104.

Moore, Harry. "Poet Frost's Letters are Bright, Salty," [newspaper review, source unknown]

Nordell, Roderick. "Frost: 'Turning Up Somewhere Else'," *Christian Science Monitor*, September 12, 1963, p. 13. Also contains a mention of a Frost Poetry award set up by the Poetry Society of America.

[Lynen, John. *The Pastoral Art of Robert Frost*]

Thompson, Lawrance. "Nature's Bard Rediscovered," *Saturday Review*, vol. 43, July 2, 1960. p. 22.

[Mertins, Louis. *Robert Frost: Life and Talks-Walking*]

Scott, Winfield Townley. "First-Hand Report," *New York Times Book Review*, September 12, 1965. p. 10.

[Morrison, Kathleen. *Robert Frost—a Pictorial Chronicle*]

Howes, Victor. "Poet of America," *The Christian Science Monitor*, September 25, 1974. p. 11.

Skow, John. "The Roads Taken," *Time*, August 12, 1974. p. 74.

[Nitchie, George. *Human Values in the Poetry of Robert Frost: A Study of a Poet's Convictions*]

Thompson, Lawrance. with review of Lynen's *The Pastoral Art of Robert Frost.*

[Poirier, Richard. *Robert Frost: the Work of Knowing*]

Howe, Irving. "The Poet of Home," *New York Times Book Review*, October 30, 1977. p. 7+. [Note by FPP: an excellent review of an important book]

[Reeve, F. D. *Robert Frost in Russia*]

Poore, Charles. "In Ten Summer Days Robert Frost Shook Russia," *New York Times*, March 24, 1964.

[Sergeant, Elizabeth Shepley. *Robert Frost: The Trial by Existence*]

Miller, Perry. "Robert Frost: His Early Ordeal and Ultimate Triumph," *New York Herald Tribune Book Review*, June 19, 1960. pp. 1+. [Note by FPP: an important review].

Scott, Winfield Townley. "A Complex, Simple Man as Yankee as the Flag," *New York Times Book Review*, June 19, 1960. p. 1+.

Thompson, Lawrance. with review of Lynen's *The Pastoral Art of Robert Frost.*

[Squires, Radcliffe. *The Major Themes of Robert Frost*]

Thompson, Lawrance. with review of Brower's *The Poetry of Robert Frost.*

[ad with a quotes from a number of reviews of the book], *New York Times Book Review*, May 26, 1963. p. 17.

[Thompson, Lawrance. *Robert Frost: The Early Years, 1874-1915*]

Fuller, Edmund. "Frost Biography Avoids His 'Little Falsehoods'," *Wall Street Journal*, November 22, 1966.

Lask, Thomas. "The Artist as a Young Man," *New York Times*, November 1, 1966.

Maddocks, Melvin. "Behind a Genial Yankee Mask," *Christian Science Monitor*, November 2, 1966. p. B-13.

Untermeyer, Louis. "The Fates Defied the Muse," *Saturday Review*, November 5, 1966. pp. 32-33.

[Thompson, Lawrance. *Robert Frost: the Years of Triumph, 1915-1938*]

Aldridge, John. "Frost Removed from Olympus," *Saturday Review*, August 15, 1970. pp. 21-23.

Jacobson, Dan. with review of Lathem's *The Poetry of Robert Frost.*

Vendler, Helen. "Robert Frost," *New York Times Book Review*, August 9, 1970. p. 1+.

Wolff, Geoffrey. "Mask of a Poet," *Newsweek*, August 24, 1970. pp. 66-67. Accompanied by letters to the editor about the review.

 [Thompson, Lawrance, editor. *Selected Letters of Robert Frost*]

Daiches, David. with review of Gould's *Robert Frost: The Aim Was Song.* "The Letters of Robert Frost," *The Boston Sunday Herald*, August 30, 1964. p. 3.

Nordell, Roderick. "The Mask of the Poet," *Christian Science Monitor*, September 3, 1964.

Prescott, Orville. "The Complexities of Robert Frost," *New York Times*, August 31, 1964.

5. Literature about Frost or drawing on his work

[Arranged alphabetically by author]

a. Poems to or about Frost

Almy, Doris E. "Robert Frost." carbon copy of typed poem. Inscribed by author to "Mildred."

Baker, Carlos. "An Old Man's Winter Night (In Memoriam: Robert Frost)." holograph poem. Signed by author. [Note by FPP: Carlos Baker was an author-scholar and Professor of English at Princeton.]

Bradley, Sam. "Four for Frost," *Shenandoah*, vol. 14, Autumn 1962. pp. 32-34.

Braithwaite, William Stanley. "To Robert Frost on His Birthday." photocopy of holograph poem and als. from Braithwaite to Frost.

Brooks, Gwendolyn. "Of Robert Frost." holograph poem. Accompanying letter from Brooks to FPP.

Derleth, August. "A Book of Poems by Robert Frost." holograph poem signed by author. Accompanying letter from Derleth to FPP.

Engle, Paul. "Robert Frost." 3000 copies distributed by the State University of Iowa Library on the occasion of Mr. Frost's visit...April 13, 1959. Library's copy inscribed by author to Stanley Fisher. [Note by FPP: see Kerr photo of April 13, 1959.]

Holmes, John. "Photograph of Robert Frost," *The Fortune Teller*, New York: Harper and Brothers, 1961. pp. 23-24.

Johnson, A. E. "To Robert Frost." newspaper clipping, [n.d.] [Note by FPP: A. E. Johnson was the Poet-in-Residence at Syracuse University for many years.]

Mas, D'Marie. "Defrosting." newspaper clipping, [n.d.]

Pastan, Linda. "Robert Frost," *Dryad*, vol. 1, Summer-Fall, 1968. p. 4.

Rosenbaum, Nathan. "To Robert Frost (On His Seventy-eighth Birthday, March 26, 1954)." typed copy and carbon copy. Accompanying correspondence with Rosenbaum.

Of Robert Frost

There is a little lightning in his eyes.
Iron at the mouth.
His brows ride neither too far
up nor down.

He is splendid. With a place to stand.

Some glowing in the Common blood.
Some specialness within.

Gwendolyn Brooks

Holograph copy of "Of Robert Frost" by Gwendolyn Brooks.

Smythe, Daniel. "A Memory of Robert Frost," *Island Advantage*, vol. 29, March 19, 1964. p. 1. Also contains an editorial on Frost and Smythe, p. 1.

Tagliabue, John. "A Bright and Weeping Student After the Lecture Tells Me What Happened." holograph poem signed by author.

Tagliabue, John. "You Know How to Prize Him, Noble New Man." holograph poem signed by author.

Tyler, Mattie R. "Robert Frost," *Congressional Record*, February 6, 1963. p. A570.

Van Egmond, Peter and Jackson Bryer. "A List of Poems To or About Robert Frost."

West of Boston: Poems from the State University of Iowa Poetry Workshop in Honor of the Visit of Robert Frost. Iowa City: the Qara Press, 1959. Accompanying correspondence from Martin Bush and Paul Engle.

Wilbur, Richard. "Seed Leaves." holograph poem. Inscribed to FPP by author and dated November 2, 1965. Also a copy of the poem in print as Wilbur's Christmas card.

b. Essays inspired by Frost poems or ideas

Beaumont, John Howland. "An Encounter," *Christian Science Monitor*, February 7, 1979. [essay centered on "A Considerable Speck"]

Cole, Charles W. "Find New Meanings," *Syracuse Post Standard Magazine*, March 13, 1960. p. 2. [essay centered on Frost's form of meditation.]

Cullander, James. "A New Yankee Works the Land," *Christian Science Monitor*, October 30, 1989. pp. 16-17. [essay centered on "After Apple-Picking"]

Daniels, Diana. "The Wind's Will," *The Christian Science Monitor*, April 16, 1968. p. 8. [essay centered on *A Boy's Will*.]

Peattie, Donald Culross. "Unfinished Business," *This Week Magazine*, August 28, 1960. p. 2. [essay centered on Frost's philosophy.]

Van Dore, Wade. "Thinking of Birches—and Robert Frost," [source unknown]. [essay centered on Frost's philosophy of nature.]

c. Correspondence concerning literature about Frost

Reed, Meredith to Mrs. Francis J. Flagg. December 2, 1963. Weymouth MA. [about his novel *Our Year Began in April* in which Frost is a character.]

6. Performances and Exhibits of Frostiana by others

Robert Frost 100

Other exhibits and performances

7. Books and articles which mention Frost briefly

WESLEYAN UNIVERSITY
MIDDLETOWN, CONNECTICUT
DEPARTMENT OF ENGLISH

Seed Leaves

for R. F.

Here something stubborn comes,
Dislodging the earth crumbs
And making crusty rubble.
It comes up bending double,
And looks like a green staple.
It could be seedling maple,
Or artichoke, or bean.
That remains to be seen.

Forced to make choice of ends,
The stalk in time unbends,
Shakes off the seed case, heaves
Aloft, and spreads two leaves
Which still display no sure
And special signature.
Toothless and fat, they keep
The oval form of sleep.

<over>

This plant would like to grow
And yet be embryo;
Increase, and yet escape
The doom of taking shape;
Be vaguely vast, and climb
To the tip end of time
With all of space to fill,
Like boundless Igdrasil
That has the stars for fruit.

But something at the root
More urgent than that urge
Bids two true leaves emerge,
And now the plant, resigned
To being self-defined
Before it can commerce
With the great universe,
Takes aim at all the sky
And starts to ramify.

Written out with pleasure
for Frank P. Piskor
2 November 1965.
Richard Wilbur

“Seed Leaves,” a poem about Frost by Richard Wilbur. This holograph copy is inscribed to Dr. Piskor by the author.

III. Material about Frost's Family

A. Isabelle Moodie Frost—Robert Frost's Mother

Painter, Clara Searle. "Mrs. Frost's Private School," *Mount Holyoke Alumnae Quarterly*, vol. 46, Winter 1963. pp. 182-3.

Painter, Clara Searle. "Of Mrs. Frost's Private School." typescript of unedited original of above article. photocopy. Accompanying letter from Painter to Mrs. Robert McClung, editor of the *Mt. Holyoke Alumnae Quarterly*. photo copy.

B. Elinor White Frost—Robert Frost's Wife

1. Material by Elinor White Frost

a. Correspondence

Mrs. Bromley
December 27. Amherst MA. photocopy.

Lesley Frost
[1918 or 1919] Postmarked Franconia NH. photocopy.
Nov. 6. [1928] London. photocopy.
December 27, 1934. Key West FL. photocopy.

Vera Harvey
[n.d.] EWF to Vera Harvey. als.
Jan. 19. EWF to Vera Harvey. Coconut Grove, FL. als.
Jan. 19. EWF to Vera Harvey. als.
Dec. 20. EWF to "Dear Girls" [Vera and Hilda Harvey]. San Antonio TX. als.
[n.d.] EWF to Vera Harvey. als.
[n.d.] EWF to Vera Harvey. als.

b. Other writings

[Excerpts from Elinor White's high school valedictory talk], *The Freethinker*, p. 129.

a. Correspondence

Piskor-Vera Harvey Correspondence

September 29, 1969. Tatham, David to FPP. Syracuse. tls.
October 9, 1969. FPP to Hilda Harvey. carbon of tl.
[n.d.] Harvey, Vera to FPP and Mrs. Piskor.
January 19, 1970. FPP to Hilda Harvey. carbon of tl.
June 17, 1970. FPP to Hilda Harvey. carbon of tl.
August 16, 1970. Harvey, Vera to FPP and Mrs. Piskor. tls.
September 23, 1970 [postmark]. Harvey, Vera to Mrs. Piskor. als.
October 13, 1970. FPP to Vera Harvey. carbon of tl.
[n.d.] Harvey, Vera to FPP. tls.
December 9, 1980. FPP to Hilda and Vera Harvey. carbon of tl.
March 16, 1981. Morrison, Kathleen [Robert Frost's secretary] to FPP. Amherst, MA. als.

Thompson Correspondence

October 27, 1946. Thompson, Lawrance to Owen D. Young. Peterborough, NH. photocopy of tls.
October 30, 1946. Young, Owen D. to Lawrance Thompson. photocopy of tl.
November 5, 1946. Thompson, Lawrance to Owen D. Young. Peterborough, NH. photocopy of tls.
November 27, 1946. Thompson, Lawrance to Owen D. Young. Peterborough, NH. photocopy of tls.
December 6, 1946. Young, Owen D. to Lawrance Thompson. photocopy of tl.
December 16, 1946. Case, Reverend Lorenzo D. to Mr. Lawrance Thompson. Brooklyn, MI. tls.

Correspondence concerning Elinor White at SLU

May 19, 1939. Newdick, Robert to Laurens Seelye. photocopy of tls.
June 2, 1939. Ellsworth, Richard to Robert Newdick. photocopy of tl.
November 12, 1946. Ellsworth, Richard to Owen D. Young. photocopy of tls.
March 11, 1963. Brown, J. Moreau to Harold Baily. photocopy of tls.
[n.d.] Andrew Peters. photocopy of memo responding to above.
May 12, 1971. Jamieson, Paul to David Powers. tls.
May 12, 1971. Young, Richard to David Powers. tls.

Kappa Kappa Gamma sorority at St. Lawrence University, 1895. Elinor White is seated on the grass, just to the left of the stairs, looking down. [Courtesy of St. Lawrence University archives]

b. Miscellaneous St. Lawrence-related materials

Photograph of Elinor White's home during her years at St. Lawrence University—Mrs. Lewis' rooming house, located on corner of Miner and Pine.

Other miscellaneous items

C. Lesley Frost Ballantine—Frost's Daughter

1. Material by Lesley Frost Ballantine

a. Correspondence

Dorothy and Paul Hatch. Accompanying letter from Mrs. Hatch to FPP.

December 1965. LFB to Dorothy Hatch. Postcard with photographs of Frost Homestead at Derry NH. autograph note by LFB.

[December] 1967. LFB to Mr. and Mrs. Paul Hatch. Christmas card with photograph of Frost's poem "Christmas Trees" illustrated by LFB.

New York Times Book Review

September 27, 1970. LFB to Editor of NY Times Book Review. Reaction to Lawrance Thompson's biography of RF.

Dr. Frank Piskor

[December] 1964. LFB to FPP and Mrs. Piskor. Christmas card with illustration from *Going on Two*. Inscription by LFB.

[December] 1968. LFB to FPP. Christmas card with inscription by LFB.

[December] 1970. LFB to FPP Christmas card with photograph of Robert Frost Homestead. One copy with inscription by LFB.

[June] 1970. LFB to FPP. Segovia, Spain. als.

December 28, 1971. LFB to FPP. New York NY. als. with signed illustrated copy of Frost's poem "An Empty Threat."

February 8, 1973. LFB to FPP. New York NY. autograph postcard.

[n.d.] LFB to FPP. Christmas card. Inscription by LFB.

David Tatham.

Collection of correspondence, dating from the late 1960s and early 1970s, between LFB and Tatham which he donated to Syracuse University. Photocopies. Accompanying letter from Tatham to FPP about collection.

b. Interviews

"An Interview with Lesley Frost," *Yankee Magazine*, December 1963, pp. 66+.

"North of Boston," *Boston Globe Magazine*, March 6, 1966, pp. 6+.

Interview with Lesley Frost Ballantine (May 25, 1971) by C. Webster Wheelock as broadcast on KSLU. [Magnetic tape. Shelved with other media materials from the collection. See page 154.]

c. Articles and Poems

"First Flight," reprinted in *The American Way*, February [1976?], p. 39. Originally appeared in *The Rockford-Register Republic*, Friday, March 1, 1935. Photocopy.

"Our Family Christmas," *Redbook*, December, 1963, vol. 122, pp. 45, 97-98. Photocopy.

"Robert Frost Remembered," *The American Way*, vol. 7, March 1974. pp. 12-17.

"Certain Intensities," *Ball State University Forum*, vol. 15, Summer 1974. pp. 3-8.

d. Performances

Derry Down Derry: a Narrative Reading by Lesley Frost of Poems by Robert Frost. Folkways records FL 9733. [Shelved with other media materials from the collection. See page 153.]

e. Information relating to *New Hampshire's Child*

2. Material about Lesley Frost Ballantine

a. Correspondence

September 28, 1966. Applegate, Howard to FPP. Syracuse NY. tls.
February 27, 1968. Tatham, David to FPP. Syracuse NY. tls.
June 1, 1971. Blackford, Benjamin to Duane Dittman. tls. [Note by FPP: Blackford was a trustee of SLU (and a graduate) related to the Frost Family. Dittman was our chief development officer]
July 7, 1971. Dittman, Duane to Benjamin Blackford. tls.

b. Articles

Ehblich, Phyllis, "Love of Poetry is a Family Tradition," *New York Times*, November 14, 1962.
Hoffman, Marilyn. "Restoring Childhood Farm Home," March 17, 1967. clipping from unknown newspaper.
"A Little Journey to the Home of a Donor," *Bulletin of the Society for the Libraries of New York University*, No. 72, Special Supplement. [May 1968] Two of SLU's copies have holograph marginal notes by Lesley Frost Ballantine. One is signed. Biographical piece on Lesley Frost Ballantine.
Bulletin of the Society for the Libraries of New York University, No. 75, Special Supplement. [May 1969] One of SLU's copies signed by Lesley Frost. Concerns the unveiling of a bust of Robert Frost.
"Robert Frost was Her Schoolmaster," *Washington Post*, April 30, 1970.

c. Material relating to Escuela de la Tahona

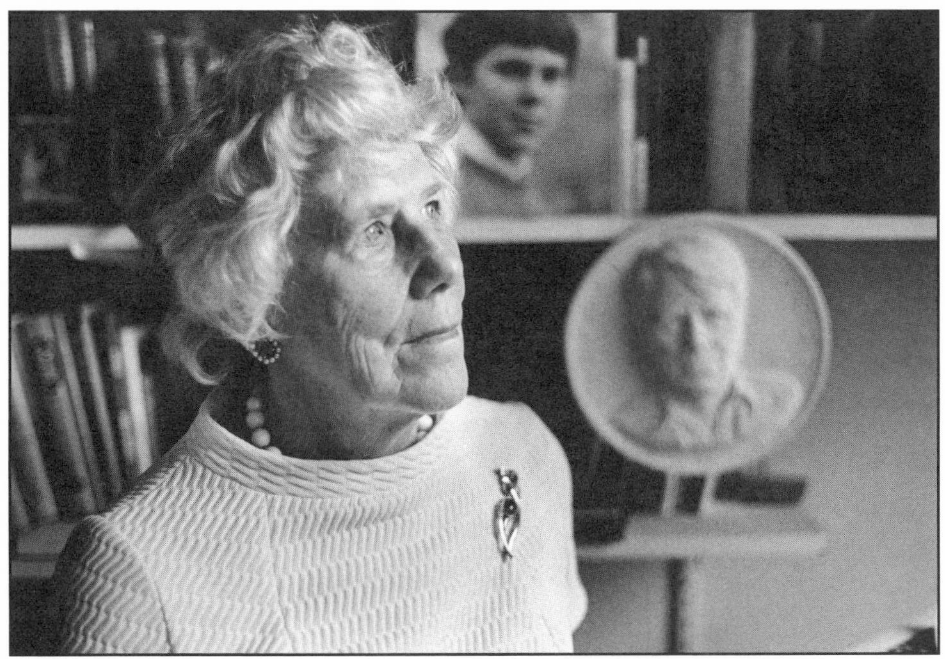

Lesley Frost Ballantine, 1971, photographed by David Powers.

d. Photographs

Photos by David Powers
    4 contact sheets, three with negatives, of photos from the SLU Frost exhibit, 1971. Accompanying letter by Powers.
        12 prints from these sheets
        3 copies of a photograph with accompanying letter
        Lesley Frost Ballantine
Photo of SLU Frost exhibit, 1971 and accompanying newspaper clipping

e. Miscellaneous

D. Lesley Francis Material—Frost's Granddaughter

1. Material by Lesley Francis

a. Correspondence

Christmas, 1992. Lesley Francis to FPP. Arlington VA.
February 10, 1993. Lesley Francis to FPP. Arlington VA.

b. Articles

"Robert Frost and the Majesty of Stones upon Stones," *Journal of Modern Literature*, vol. 9, 1981, pp. 3-26.

"'Imperfectly Academic': Robert Frost and Harvard," *Harvard Magazine*, March-April 1984, pp. 51-56.

"Robert Frost and Susan Hayes Ward," *The Massachusetts Review*, vol. 26, Summer-Autumn 1985, pp. 341-350.

"A Decade of 'Stirring Times': Robert Frost and Amy Lowell," *The New England Quarterly*, vol. 59, December 1986, pp. 508-522.

"Between Poets: Robert Frost and Harriet Monroe," *The South Carolina Review*, vol. 19, Summer 1987, pp. 2-13.

"Robert Frost and Helen Thomas Revisited," *Dartmouth College Library Bulletin*, vol. 32, November 1991, pp. 10-17.

2. Material about Lesley Francis

Vita with accompanying letter by Lesley Francis.

E. Elinor Wilber Material—Frost's Granddaughter

F. Robert L. Frost Material—Frost's Great-grandson

G. Frost Family Homes

a. Homes in England

General

- 7 drawings by Vaughn Bode of Frost's English residences. Photographic prints. Accompanying letter from David Tatham.
- Tatham, David. *Robert Frost's England.* [Note by FPP: a unique photographic reference. This is one of two copies—three at most.]

Beaconsfield, England

Dymock, England [Little Iddens]

- Includes photocopy of The Reverend Canon J. E. Gethyn-Jones' manuscript for "I Have Come by the Highway Home."

Derry Farm, NH
Franconia, NH
Gainesville, FL
Ossippee Mountain, NH
Ripton, VT
Shaftsbury, VT

IV. Material about Frost's friends

A. Philip Booth

1. Biographical information

2. Correspondence with Dr. Piskor

[Note by FPP on letter of September 9, 1972: an important letter. See Frost's letter to me on Philip Booth, p. 102.]

3. Articles by Booth about Frost

[arranged chronologically]

"Journey Out of a Dark Forest," *New York Times Book Review*, March 25, 1962. pp. 1+. Accompanied by working draft of the review and by a letter to FPP about writing the review.

"Los Poemas de Robert Frost," *Comentario*, Vol. 9, March-April 1963. pp. 2+.

"Frost's 'Constellations of Intention': "The Figure a Poem Makes'," *Christian Science Monitor*, April 25, 1963. p. 11. [review of *The Poetry of Robert Frost*, by Reuben A. Brower.]

"A Weakness for Poetry," foreword to *Syracuse Poems, 1965*. pp. v-viii. Library's copy inscribed to FPP by Booth. Accompanied by letter to FPP and carbon copy of typescript of foreword and by galley proofs of the entire book.

"Coming to Terms," foreword to *Syracuse Poems, 1973*. pp. v-viii. Library's copy is number 1 of 500. Library's copy inscribed to FPP by Booth.

4. Items in print by Booth—not about Frost

"Route 66—Television on the Road Toward People," *Television Quarterly*, vol. 2, Winter, 1963. pp. 5-12.

"Four Poems," *The Virginia Quarterly Review*, vol. 40, Summer 1964. pp. 407-410. Also contains a short statement of future plans on p. xcii and an announcement of the Emily Clark Balch Prize on p. xv.

"The Varieties of Poetic Experience," *Shenandoah*, vol. 15, Summer 1964. pp. 62-69. [review of *The Quarry*, by Richard Eberhart.]

"Hard Country," broadside. Library's copy is number 2 of 75. Hand-printed by the Lowell House Printers, 1967. Illustrated by Fred Fiske. Library's copy is inscribed by Booth to FPP and signed by Fiske.

5. Items in manuscript by Booth—not about Frost

"Adam" [Note by FPP: April 1963.]

"Stone"

6. Articles about Booth's poetry

Dickey, James. "Neither Maddeningly Genteel Nor Bawling," *New York Times Book Review*, December 24, 1961. pp. 4-5. [review of *The Islanders*, by Booth.]

"In the Twilight of an Old Order, the Promising New Poets," *The National Observer*, April 8, 1963. p. 20.

B. Edward and Helen Thomas

1. Magazine articles

Evans, William. "Robert Frost and Helen Thomas: Five Revealing Letters (Pt. 2)," *Dartmouth College Library Bulletin*, vol. 30, April 1990. pp. 38-44.

Farjeon, Eleanor. "Edward Thomas and Robert Frost," *The London Magazine*, vol. 1, May 1954. pp. 50-61.

Francis, Lesley. "Robert Frost and Helen Thomas Revisited," *Dartmouth College Library Bulletin*, vol. 32, November 1991. pp. 10-17. [Shelved with Lesley Francis material. See page 138.]

Powell, Anthony. "From Hack to War Poet," newspaper clipping from a London paper.

Autograph note by Thomas.
Recording of Helen Thomas reading the poems of Edward Thomas. Accompanying correspondence. [Recording shelved with other media material from the collection. See page 154.]
Information on Thomas window in Church of St. James the Greater at Eastbury

C. Other persons connected to Frost

[Note by FPP: the Lowell and Stork items on Pound are important—indirectly related to Frost because of the Frost-Pound relationship.]

V. Frost organizations

A. California Friends of Frost

Luncheon on 90th anniversary of Frost's birth, March 26, 1964
Information on "Once by the Pacific," a film produced in 1970 by the Friends about Frost's California years
Miscellaneous information about the California Friends of Frost

B. Robert Frost Society

Newsletters
- Summer 1988 in *South Carolina Review*, vol. 21, Fall 1988. pp. 60-64.
- Summer 1989 in *South Carolina Review*, vol. 22, Fall 1989. pp. 152-159.
- Summer 1990 in *South Carolina Review*, vol. 23, Fall 1990. pp. 136-149.

VI. Bibliographic information about the collection

A. General Frost bibliographies

B. Material related to specific items in this collection

1. The Christmas cards

Blankman, Edward J. "Story of a Christmas Card," *St. Lawrence Bulletin*, vol. 26, Fall 1967. pp. 4-5.

Data on Frost Christmas card imprints
Correspondence about Lesley Frost Ballantine's gift of Christmas cards
Information on various displays of Christmas cards

2. The Four Beliefs—PS 3511. R94 F6

Brown, Bette Anne. *The Religious Implications of Robert Frost's Masques.* typescript of thesis.

Frost, Robert. "Education by Poetry," *Amherst Graduate Quarterly*, vol. 20, February, 1931. pp. 75-85.

Frost, Robert. *An Uncompleted Revision of "Education by Poetry".* keepsake from a Frost gathering held at Dartmouth College, July 3, 1966.

Lathem, Edward Connery to FPP. February 18, 1964. Hanover, NH. tls. [concerns FPP's annotated copy of *The Four Beliefs*.]

Nash, Ray. calligraphed envelope by Nash in which he sent the printing of *The Four Beliefs*. [Note by FPP: this is printing is one of a kind.]

Ohl, Ronald. "One Memory of a Star Splitter," *This*, March 1965. pp. 4-6.

Book dealers' catalogs

Black Sun Press—p. 24. Accompanying letter from FPP.

House of Books—p. 18. [Note by FPP: early offering of *The Four Beliefs*.]

3. Individual Titles—information or association items

Clymer, William. *Robert Frost, a Bibliography*. PS 3511.R94 Z575

Frost, Robert. *A Boy's Will*. PS 3511.R94 B6 1934

Frost, Robert. *In the Clearing*. PS 3511. R94 I5 1962a

Frost, Robert. *In the Clearing*. PS 3511. R94 I5 1962c

typescript of Robert Graves' introduction with holograph corrections

Frost, Robert. *Sermon*. PS 3511.R94 S4 1947

Grade, Arnold. *A Robert Frost Folio*. PS 3511.R94 Z683

Hall, Donald. *An Evening's Frost*. PS 3515.A3152 E9

Tatham, David. *A Poet Recognized*. PS 3511.R94 Z9268 1969

Tatham, David. *Robert Frost's White Mountains*. PS 3511.R94 Z929 1974

Tkatch, Meyer Ziml. *Lider un Poemes*. PS 3511.R94 A58 1965

Lehtedel Sammuja. PS 3511.R94 .A53 1965

C. Dr. Piskor's correspondence about the collection

Correspondence with Daniel Smythe

Other Correspondence
1957-1968
[Note by FPP on November 16, 1966 letter of Harry Owen: Harry Goddard Owen was a professor at Middlebury. Also responsible at one point for Bread Loaf writers' school. Finally dean of Rutgers College. He knew Frost well.]
SLU Years [Note by FPP on these files: an organized picture of collecting during the SLU years. The whole file really reflects our interest in building a collection with a Frost Family focus and Lesley's positive response.]
1970
[Note by FPP on September 23, 1970 letter of Donald Bean: Dr. Bean was the long-time editor of the University of Chicago Press until SU "stole" him.]
1971
1972
1973-1974
1975-1978
1980-

D. Frost material in other collections

1. Private collectors

Mrs. George Parks

2. Colleges and universities

Boston University
Dartmouth
Indiana University
Middlebury College
New York University
Plymouth State College
Syracuse University
[Note by FPP on clipping about the Hudson volume of *North of Boston*: I bought this item and some proofs of *A Boy's Will* for Syracuse University in a Sotheby sale in London through House of Books (open bid). The poem "To

E. T." was written out by Mr. Frost at my request on a trip to Ripton VT. When Mr. Frost was at SU in 1959, he added the reference to the Arents Room.]

University of New Hampshire
University of Texas
University of Virginia

3. Other libraries

Library of Congress

E. Booksellers catalogs

[arranged chronologically]

Notes by Dr. Piskor:

Parke-Bernet Galleries catalog of December 1950—"important because of Bernheimer items in my collection."

House of Books 50th Anniversary Catalog—"important because of the introduction which deals with the history of the firm from 1930 to 1960."

Sotheby Sale catalog of June 19, 1962—"describes the copy of *North of Boston* in the Arents Room at Syracuse University."

F. Publisher's ads, jackets, etc. for Frost titles

Books by Frost
Books about Frost

[Note by FPP on jacket for *Robert Frost: A Study in Sensibility and Common Sense* by Gorham Munson: the first critical study.]

[Note by FPP on the New Dresden Press prospectus: the press did not survive. The book is very rare now.]

VII. Miscellany

A. Frost in art

1. Photographic prints

a. Frost Family Photograph Album

The items in this subseries are from a black notebook of family photographs donated by Lesley Frost Ballantine. The labels on the envelopes are the ones that she used for the photos in the book and her original labels are kept with the collection.

Elinor Frost—photo of a painting by J. Chapin
Robert Frost—England, 1913
Isabelle (Belle) Moodie Frost—San Francisco, circa 1875
Robert Frost—San Francisco, 1874. 6 mo.
William Prescott Frost—San Francisco
Lawrence MA High School
Tremont Street House. See *Robert Frost: Trial by Existence*—Sergeant
Robert Frost—high school graduation, 1892
Elinor Miriam White—St. Lawrence University
Elinor Miriam White—St. Lawrence University
Mrs. W.P. Frost's private school—Salem, NH, 1886-87. Robert with hat, Jeannie—long hair, front row
Receipt to Robert Frost from Town of Derry NH for taxes. July 1, 1903. photocopy.
Short typed piece about a doll with handwritten note "Lesley, circa 1903—R.F." photocopy.
Robert Frost—Franconia, 1916
"The Stone House"—S. Shaftsbury, VT
The Frost Family with Pony
Bethlehem NH—Lynch Farm, 1908
Robert and Elinor Frost—Plymouth NH, 1912
[Unlabeled photo of four children—three girls and a boy]
Hotel where Frosts "landed" in 1912
"Little Iddens"—Leadington. The Frosts' 2d home in England, 1914
Little Iddens—Ledbury [sic], Glos., England. Photographed 22 May 1966 by David Tatham

Elinor Miriam White
at St. Lawrence University.

Frost in England, 1913.

The Frost children at Plymouth, NH, 1911. Left to right: Marjorie, Lesley, Carol and Irma.

The Frost Family, 1916-17. Taken on
Webster Farm. George Brown
Collection—Plymouth College Library
Robert Frost [and] Carrol Frost—
Franconia, 1916-17
Frost Home, 1900-09.
On Route 28, Derry, NH
The Derry Farm, 1900-1909
The Derry Farm, 1900-1909
The Derry Farm, 1900-1909
Edward Thomas—England, 1914
Robert Frost—1915
"The Franconia Stove"—1916
Carrol Frost—S. Shaftsbury, VT, stone house
Marjorie Frost—S. Shaftsbury, VT, stone house
Picnic, 1920—Robert Frost, Elinor Frost, Jean Starr Untermeyer
"The Gully"—S. Shaftsbury, VT
Robert Frost—1935
Robert Frost, 1923. Photograph of a painting by Leon Makielski, Ann Arbor
Elinor Frost—Rockford College, 1935
Robert and Elinor—Longs Peak, Colorado, 1932

Frost with his son Carol at Franconia, 1916-17.

Marjorie Frost (Mrs. Willard Fraser).

Irma Frost (Mrs. John Payne Cone).

Lesley Frost, 1938.

Willard and Robin Fraser—1942
Irma Frost—Mrs. John Payne Cone
Marjorie Frost—Mrs. Willard Fraser
Carrol Frost—Gainesville, Florida, 1938
Lesley Frost—1938
Lesley Frost
Sunset Ave. House—Amherst, 1930-38

b. Photos by David Tatham

Ripton VT cabin of Frost. Accompanying letter from David Tatham.
Amherst-related photos
Album of photos and comments on the Franconia Mountains and Frost 1964.

c. Photos used in article by Walter Carroll

6 photographs (2 prints of each) by Howard Schmitt with negatives.

5 photographs by Judith Buck

Carroll, Walter. "Howard Schmitt, Friend and Collector—Where Two Roads Converge: Forty-Six Degrees and Frost." *Post-Standard Sunday Magazine.* August 25, 1963 pp. 4-5, 7-8.

d. Other Photos of Frost

Frost in the garden of the Warden at Wadham College, Oxford. December 10, 1957. 2 slides. Accompanying letter from Prof. Lawrance Thompson.

Frost and Dr. Masayoski Higashiyama at Middlebury. 1957.

Frost and Professor Cook at Middlebury. Accompanying letters from George Huban.

Procession at academic convocation at Syracuse. April 21, 1959.

Frost and Daniel Smythe at Bread Loaf. Original and enlargement.

Frost and unknown man from Dartmouth. Accompanying letter from E. H. Henry.

Frost and Walter Hard at Manchester, VT.

Frost and Elbert Snow.

Frost at Ripton VT. June 3, 1962. Accompanying letter from Robert Cotner.

Frost. Photographed in 1960 by Daniel Smythe. Small original, two enlargements, and negative.

Frost. Photographed by I. S. Cole.

Frost. Photographed in 1961 by Ruth Archer.

Frost. [Note FPP: May have been used to advertise either "In the Clearing" or "A Further Range."]

Frost leaving the stage after a reading at University of Iowa. Photographed by George Kern. [Note by FPP: this photograph won a prize.]

Frost. Photographed by Clara Sipprell. Accompanied by a letter from Clara Sipprell about Frost and a copy of Vermont Life magazine in which there is a reproduction of the photograph. Also accompanied by a newspaper copy of the photo.

Frost

Frost

Prize-winning photograph by George Kern of Frost leaving the stage after a reading at University of Iowa.

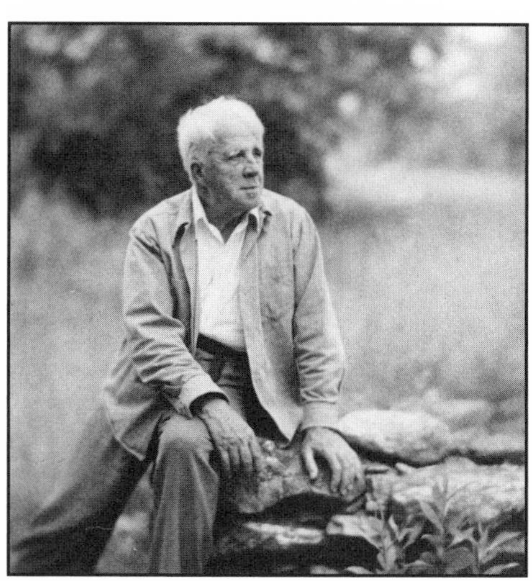

Frost, photographed by Clara Sipprell.

e. Other Photographs of Frost Family and Frost Homes

Frost Family

Photo of Frost and children playing pick-up-sticks

Homes of Frost at South Shaftsbury VT: The Stone House (Route 7) and The Gully (East Road). 2 prints. Accompanying card quoting from letter of Mrs. Arthur Davids.

2. Published photos of Frost

"Robert Frost," *New York Herald Tribune Weekly Book Review*, February 14, 1943. [photoessay on Frost].

Keepsake printing from Holt, Rinehart and Winston of "The Gift Outright" with photo of Frost reciting it at the inauguration of John F. Kennedy.

Postcard with photo of Frost at Ripton VT. [Note by FPP: the message on the card, identifying Ripton as Frost's birthplace, is incorrect; he was born in San Francisco.]

Postcard with photo of Frost's cabin at Ripton VT.

Photo of Frost with the John Glenns and the John Kennedys in Robert Kennedy campaign ad

Photos in periodicals—articles not otherwise about Frost

3. Representations of Frost in other forms of art

Original caricature of Frost by Jack Rosen. Signed by Frost. Accompanying letter from Jack Rosen.

Original pen and ink drawing of Frost by Tom Holloway. 1963.

Marlow, James. "Frost—Both Man and Myth," *Herald American STARS Magazine*. February 17, 1963, p. 2. Cover has picture of Frost. Accompanied by original mockup for the cover art.

Original art work for cover of Frost issue of *Writer's Digest*. April 1963. Accompanying correspondence about the art work.

"Portrait of Robert Frost," a lithograph by Grant Reynard made from a life drawing done at Middlebury. Accompanying *Bulletin* of the Montclair Art Museum for May 1966 telling about Reynard.

Photoengraving of Frost by J. J. Lankes. Accompanying note by Corinne (Mrs. Arthur Davids.)

Caricature of Frost by Oscar Berger on cover of the *Bulletin* of The Poetry Society of America for 1962.

Poster with text of "Stopping by Woods on a Snowy Evening" and a painting of Frost.

Picture of Frost torn from autograph dealer's catalog.

Bookmark with etching of Frost on one side and biographical information on the other.

Print reproductions of busts—Walter Hancock, Joseph Brown, Leo Cherne.

Reproductions of paintings

- Photo of portrait in Mayer Collection. Accompanying note by Ed Weiss.
- Photo of Ferdinand Warren with his portrait of Frost at Agnes Scott College.
- Photos and clippings about Rosamond Coolidge portrait of Frost at Curry College.
- *American Portraits between the Fairs, 1939-1964*. Exhibition catalog from Portraits, Inc. Gardner Cox portrait of Frost is on the cover. Accompanied by May 1964 issue of *The Art Gallery* with an ad for the catalog on p. 4.
- Newspaper clipping with reproduction of portrait by Gardner Cox.
- Color reproduction of portrait by Gardner Cox.

Robert Frost
Whether to seek a scientific sky
Or wait and go to Heaven
when they die.
In other words to wager their
reliance
On plain religion or religious
science

Original caricature of Frost by Jack Rosen. Signed by Frost.

Medals and other objects

- Robert Frost Vermont Freedom and Unity Medal. Medal, news clipping, and photograph.
- "The Gift Outright" Medal presented to Frost on his 88th birthday by President John F. Kennedy. Medal and accompanying newspaper clippings and letter by Corinne (Mrs. Arthur) Davids.
- California Friends of Robert Frost. Medal and accompanying correspondence from G. William Gahagan.
- California Friends of Robert Frost. Keychain with Robert Frost stamp.

Robert Frost Vermont Freedom and Unity Medal.

Print of "Stopping by Woods on a Snowy Evening" in calligraphy by Bette McNear. Accompanying correspondence with McNear.

Illustration of "The Road Not Taken" in Tolley, William. *The Hope of the Future: Chancellor's Address to Freshmen.* Hendricks Chapel, September 20, 1961. center pages.

Christmas cards from Dartmouth with woodcuts by J.J. Lankes

- Frost's farm, "The Gully"
- "Robert Frost's Pasture, S. Shaftsbury"
- Cards made from woodcuts from Frost poems
  - "Christmas Dawn"
  - "Big Tree"
  - "After Apple Picking"
- "The Gully Hayfield, Robert Frost's Farm, South Shaftsbury, Vermont, 1929."
- "Robert Frost's South Shaftsbury, Vermont, house. Insert in one of the cards says this was Lankes' last Christmas card. Accompanying letter from Herbert West.

Frost Bookplates. Accompanying letters from Corinne (Mrs. Arthur) Davids.

Cartoons

Wood engraving by J.J. Lankes of Frost's South Shaftsbury house, used as a Christmas card by the Friends of Dartmouth Library.

MEDIA

Cassette Recordings

Afternoon Tribute to Robert Frost.
[S.l.: s.n.], n.d.
Participants: Governor of New Hampshire Melvin Thompson, Lesley Frost Ballantine, Frank P. Piskor, John Dickey, and former Governor of New Hampshire Sherman Adams.

Amherst College Convocation and Library Ground Breaking.
Amherst, MA: WAMF/WFCR, Amherst College, November 14, 1963.
Address by Archibald MacLeish; Groundbreaking remarks by John F. Kennedy.

The Common Frost.
New London, NH: Colby-Sawyer College, April 22, 1982.
Rufus Porter Lecture presented by James Cox, Avalon Professor of Humanities at Dartmouth College.

Derry Down Derry. A Narrative Reading by Lesley Frost of Poems by Robert Frost (including selections from "You Come Too").
New York: Folkways Records, c1961.
"To the Elinor Frost Collection at St. Lawrence University from Lesley Frost May 25, 1971."

The Enjoyment of Poetry.
[S.l.: s.n.], 1955.
"Princeton '55: An Exploration into Education through Television" with Lawrance Thompson, Professor of English, analyzing "The Witch of Coos," and joined by Robert Frost speaking as "the maker of poetry."

[156] *The Drama of Poetry.*
Colorado: N.A.E.B. Tape Network, n.d.
Originally produced at the University of Wisconsin, WHA, with Emeritus Professor of English Harry Glickson as commentator, assisted by the Radio Hall Players. Performance in honor of Frost's 75th Birthday [1950].

In Memory of Robert Frost.
Hanover, NH: WDCR, Dartmouth College Radio, March 6, 1963.
Professor Herbert F. West, speaker. Includes Frank Dobie's tribute to Robert Frost, Robert Graves' Tribute to Robert Frost, and selections from the *London Times* and other obituaries in England. Mentions "Frank Piskor at Syracuse" regarding collections.

Invitation to Learning.
[S.l.]: CBS, May 24, 1962.
"A critical discussion of the poetry of Robert Frost" by George Carruthers with John Ciardi, poet and director of the Bread Loaf School of English Writers, and Professor Lawrance Thompson, Princeton University.

Lesley Frost Ballantine Interview.
[S.l.: s.n.], October 17, 1987.
Interviewed by Martha Deane on WOR Radio.

Lesley Frost Ballantine Interview.
[S.l.: s.n.], May 25, 1971.
Interviewed by C. Webster Wheelock on radio station KSLU.

Meet the Press.
[S.l.: s.n.], December 25, 1955.
Robert Frost meets with A. T. Baker (*Time* magazine), Inez Robb (Scripps Howard Newspapers), Norman Cousins (*Saturday Review*), with Lawrence Spivak, moderator.

The Poems of Edward Thomas Introduced and Read by Helen Thomas.
Newbury, Eng: Kennet Recordings, May 1965.

The Poems of Robert Lee Frost.
Syracuse, NY: Syracuse University, May 8, 1963.
Student production, Co-Producers/Directors Ann Burnat '64, Bill Ledger '64.

Poetic Patterns.
[S.l.]: Oregon School of the Air, Radio Station KOAC, n.d.
Sheldon Goldstein, reader and commentator in a program on narrative poetry. Features "Death of the Hired Man."

Robert Frost Address at Phillips Exeter, October 11, 1956.
The Library, Phillips Exeter Academy, Exeter, New Hampshire.
See above p. 117, "Frost and Education - Frost and Other Educational Institutions - Exeter" for a printed version of this address.

Robert Frost at the University of Massachusetts.
Readings with Commentary.
[S.l.]: University of Massachusetts, October 25, 1961.
Memorial lectures founded in 1959 to honor University of Massachusetts W.W.II alumni who died in the war. Frost's appearance sponsored by the University of Massachusetts War Memorial Committee.

Robert Frost Commemorative Ceremony.
Derry, NH: [s.n.], n.d.
Ceremony related to commemorative stamp.

Robert Frost Honorary Degree.
Syracuse, NY: Syracuse University, Spring 1959.

Robert Frost Lecture at State University of Iowa.
[S.l.]: State University of Iowa, April 13, 1959.
Introduction by the poet Paul Engle, Poet in Residence.

Robert Frost Press Conference.
Syracuse, NY: Syracuse University, Spring 1959.
Pre-convocation press conference with representatives from central New York newspapers, before the ceremony at which Frost received an honorary degree.

Robert Frost Reading at Bread Loaf.
Ripton, VT: Bread Loaf School of English, July 5, 1954.
Includes informal question-and-answer period in Bread Loaf Barn on evening of August 2, 1954, and beginning of a talk and reading at Bread Loaf Writer's Conference on August, 26, 1954 after his return from Brazil.

Robert Frost, "The Importance of Separateness."
Chapel Hill, NC: University of North Carolina Communication Center, February 3, 1960.
First in the series, "Listen America." Director, John Clayton. Producer, John Ely. NAEP Radio Network.

Robert Frost. Recitation of His Poems.
Syracuse, NY: Syracuse University Audio Archives, March 4, 1932.
Filtered and equalized by Walter L. Welch, Curator and Director, December 6, 1966.

Robert Penn Warren Recorded on National Public Radio.
[S.l.: s.n.], April 5 and 12, 1974.
The National Endowment for the Humanities Jefferson Lectures in the Humanities.

Tribute to Robert Frost.
[S.l.]: NBC Radio, January 29, 1963.
Leon Pierson host and narrator. Readings of "Birches," "The Gift Outright," "Stopping by Woods on a Snowy Evening." Reflections on Nikita Khrushchev.

Tribute to Robert Frost.
[S.l.]: WGBH, February 17, 1963.
Johnson Chapel Memorial Service, Amherst College, Amherst, MA. Service conducted by Bishop Henry W. Thompson, Bishop of Southern Ohio. Includes tribute by Mark Van Doren. For print copy of text SEE "Tributes to Frost After His Death," p. 118.

Video Recordings

Robert Frost.
Santa Barbara, CA: Annenberg/CPB Project, n.d.
Part of the "Voices and Visions" project; one of thirteen programs featuring American poets. (60 minutes)

Robert Frost: Versed in Country Things.
New Hampshire: New Hampshire Public Television, October 23, 1989.
Frost documentary. (30 minutes)

One of 1,000 copies
printed by Salina Press, Manlius, New York, and bound by The Riverside Group, Rochester, New York. Goudy types are used throughout. The text is printed on Mohawk Superfine; the cover, printed letterpress by Jim Benvenuto, is on Neenah Environment 25. The portrait of Robert Frost which appears on the cover and title page was specially commissioned for this project and is the work of wood engraver Gregory Lago.